Understanding and Managing Children's Be
through Group Work
Ages 7–11

Understanding and Managing Children's Behaviour provides the reader with an insight into children's emotional well-being and helps them to understand what and how children communicate and how to respond in a way that provides positive messages, increases their emotional vocabulary and encourages them to change their behaviour. It provides an alternative and effective child-centred way of managing children's behaviour through introducing the concept of reflective language and other tools, equipping staff with new skills that are transferable across the school in any role.

The book is divided into two sections, enabling the reader to link theory with practice. The first section takes the reader on a journey to help them understand the different factors that influence children's behaviour. The second section of the book focuses on the group work programmes, how they can be used, their value and the impact they can have on children and the school as a whole. The activities in the group work programmes explore the concept of using reflective language as a behaviour management tool and are designed to motivate and build confidence, self-esteem and resilience. Useful pedagogical features throughout the book include:

- practitioner and classroom management tips and reflective tasks;
- strategies and practical ideas for staff to use to help them engage more deeply with the contents of the book;
- flexible, tried and tested group work programmes designed to promote inclusion rather than exclusion;
- clear step-by-step instructions for delivering the group work programmes;
- case studies showing behaviour examples with detailed explanations for the behaviour and strategies to respond to it.

This book is aimed at all primary school staff, especially teaching assistants, learning mentors and family workers who can deliver the group work programmes. It is also recommended reading for SENCOs and trainee teachers, and will be useful for therapists who work with children and are looking at delivering other approaches in their work.

Cath Hunter is a therapeutic consultant, trainer and play therapist and has thirty years' experience of working with children, staff and families. Her academic experience includes lecturing on childcare and play work at City College Manchester and working as a clinical supervisor at Liverpool Hope University.

Visit the author's website at www.therapeuticfamilyinterventions.co.uk

Understanding and Managing Children's Behaviour through Group Work Ages 7–11

A child-centred programme

Cath Hunter

Routledge
Taylor & Francis Group

LONDON AND NEW YORK

First published 2013
by Routledge
2 Park Square, Milton Park, Abingdon, Oxon OX14 4RN

Simultaneously published in the USA and Canada
by Routledge
711 Third Avenue, New York, NY 10017

Routledge is an imprint of the Taylor & Francis Group, an informa business

British Library Cataloguing in Publication Data
A catalogue record for this book is available from the British Library

Library of Congress Cataloging in Publication Data
Hunter, Cath.
Understanding and managing children's behaviour through group work ages 7-11 : a child-centred programme / Cath Hunter.
pages cm
Includes bibliographical references.
ISBN 978-0-415-65626-9 (pbk.) -- ISBN 978-0-203-07803-7 (ebook) 1.
Classroom management. 2. Problem children--Behavior modification. 3.
Behavior disorders in children. I. Title.
LB3013.H84 2013
371.39'3--dc23
2012043604

ISBN: 978-0-415-65626-9 (pbk)
ISBN: 978-0-203-07803-7 (ebk)

Typeset in Helvetica by GreenGate Publishing Services, Tonbridge, Kent

Printed and bound in Great Britain by CPI Group (UK) Ltd, Croydon, CR0 4YY

For Dad

Contents

List of figures and tables

Figures

Tables

Foreword

Carol Powell

There is never an uneventful start of the day in our school and on one of these busy Tuesday mornings, Cath and I stood together watching Jack hurtle down the long and tempting expanse that is our bottom corridor. I shouted 'Jack, walk.' Cath just laughed and said 'Not yet Carol.' And what was Jack's reaction? He was oblivious to us both and carried on as if released from a spinning top. Jack, at that time, had just started in Year 1, he was five years old and had recently started play therapy with Cath.

Sadly, Jack's story, though shocking, is not unusual; born addicted to heroin and never having connected with his birth mother, he lives with his older sister on a residency order. He looked and behaved like a much younger child and spent the school day in solitary but fairly physical activity. Trying to teach Jack was rather like trying to catch water! Enter Cath; her expert advice and calm manner gave Jack space to relax and to discover himself in the safe and undirected environment of the play room. Jack engaged with Cath immediately, though she reported that she needed extra time to tidy the play room after his sessions and every time she walked him back to class he ran ahead of her and we all heard him coming!

Cath stuck with him, she gave advice to his teachers about how to teach him and spent time helping his sister learn about his needs and gently directed her in ways of meeting those needs. When specialists knee-jerked into a diagnosis of ADHD for him, Cath helped me write a letter asking them to wait for the play therapy to work its magic before medicating him.

Jack is one of our individuals with severe difficulties; his life chances were compromised before he was born but with Cath's support we are helping him to catch up. Cath has worked like this in our school and others to help children like Jack and those who are experiencing less severe but still significant challenges in life. She has worked with teachers to develop their skills and knowledge so that they can teach and interact with all children in a calm and effective manner. Her way of working and her sound advice are now accessible to many more teachers and their teams in this easy to follow and ultimately practical guide. Cath writes with authority and, as she does everything, with empathy. Her ideas are easy to implement and tried and tested – they work. She has worked in schools and knows the challenges facing many of us who are trying to provide for children who have become out of kilter with their worlds. She writes so clearly because she has experienced these challenges first hand – her methods are underpinned with specialist knowledge about how children develop and what they need to flourish.

I cannot recommend Cath's book highly enough; its purpose is to help and support those of us who are trying to get it right – it comes from a compassionate place. This book will definitely be joining our staff library.

And what of Jack now? A year on, he walks down the corridor and sits with his peers on the carpet in his classroom. He stays still long enough to listen. He is learning and making progress though he still struggles to grasp ideas that other children of his age manage to understand.

Perhaps the biggest indicator of Jack's development is that last week, as Cath and I stood on the corridor talking, he came up to her, hugged her and then in complete charge of himself, walked up to his classroom. Now he has a chance.

Carol Powell
Head teacher

Acknowledgements

I would like to express my thanks and gratitude to the following people who have helped to make this book possible:

The head teachers who employ me and demonstrate their ongoing commitment to understanding, supporting and valuing the work I carry out in their schools.

Carol Powell for her thoughtful contribution in writing the foreword.

The school staff that have the courage and capacity to think about children in a different way and implement the strategies and techniques I suggest during staff consultations and training.

The teaching assistants, learning mentors and family workers in schools who have used this programme, especially Andrea Wheeldon, Caroline Wilson, Vicki Graham and Naisen Berraies for their ongoing dedication to implementing the programmes in school and having a significant impact on the children they have worked with.

Debbie Estkowski, my supervisor, for the many years of support and wisdom she has provided.

Sue Taplin for her creative contribution to the resources section.

My friends for accepting seeing less of me and supporting me in a variety of different ways.

Jane O'Neill, because I really couldn't have done it without you.

Introduction

For many staff working in primary schools today their desire to support and encourage learning is disrupted by children who do not conform to the expectations of engaged participation in daily school life. We may know of children who have refused to follow instructions, appear to be deliberately disruptive and challenge staff. We may also know of children who are withdrawn, overly eager to please and unable to build and sustain relationships. In some schools there may only be a few children causing concern, in others there may be many. This booked is aimed at helping school staff to understand and support these children and therefore achieve their full potential at school.

The purpose of this book is to provide a greater insight into children's behaviour and enable school staff to increase their awareness of what children may be trying to communicate by their behaviour. It is aimed at encouraging different ways of thinking about children and facilitating a better understanding of their difficulties by encouraging school staff to explore the possible meanings behind children's actions. It will focus on increasing understanding of why a child may be doing something, rather than just looking at the behaviour the child is displaying. It also examines the importance of helping children with their feelings instead of just trying to get them to stop their behaviour. The book is divided into two parts to assist the reader to link the theory of supporting emotional health and well-being and improving behaviour with the practical tools to enable school staff to achieve this on a regular basis.

School staff can be confronted with children exhibiting challenging behaviour that ensures they are visible and known to school staff on a regular basis. This book is aimed at exploring the possible reasons why children may be showing these behaviours, along with providing strategies that can be implemented in class to enable them to make positive changes. It is also aimed at raising awareness of children who may be less visible and require additional support to ensure they are noticed and their needs are met. It introduces accessible and successful techniques and strategies for school staff to use to improve children's self-esteem and relational behaviour, and promote emotional health and well-being.

I hope it will encourage staff to reflect on a child's behaviour and communications in order to improve understanding and promote a greater awareness of the impact of external circumstances on their mental health and well-being. This knowledge may then affect how adults respond to children, which may in turn positively influence the relationship between staff and children. When adults are open to making small changes in the way they view and respond to children's behaviour, this can have a positive impact on children, enabling them to feel more accepted and understood. The techniques and suggestions focus on strengthening the adult–child relationship and may also enable school staff to feel more competent and confident in their role in school.

As children spend a large proportion of their lives at school, schools play a crucial role in providing a range of social experiences, as well as having a key part to play in developing resilience in children. They play a vital part in both teaching and modelling relationships and life skills to children. When children have difficult experiences outside school they may not be well equipped to manage school and engage with their learning. Schools are in an ideal position to help them with this and provide them with skills to have a successful life. This book examines the importance of considering children's individual needs and social and emotional needs, which are as important as a child's learning needs and have a huge impact on their ability to engage with their learning.

An awareness and understanding of children's emotional health and well-being is imperative for their general well-being and learning. Children's physical and emotional safety, needs and well-being need to come first and be a priority for schools in order for children to be happy, safe and secure and reach their full potential. In school we may ask children to perform tasks that may expose them or make them feel vulnerable such as reading out in class or having a part in an assembly or school play. Children need to feel safe and secure in order to do this. When a child finds it difficult to put their feelings into words they are at a disadvantage at school in terms of making and sustaining friendships and being able to access the curriculum. Children who are able to understand and express their feelings are able to achieve success at school and reach their potential more easily.

Using reflective language is a key concept in this book and in my experience is one of the most powerful tools that can change children's behaviour and set them on the path to improved mental health and well-being. The use of reflective language throughout the book, and particularly in the facilitator's notes that accompany each session, can be used with children in any context and provide a different approach to working with children. This unique and easy to use method helps to develop self-awareness, self-control and resilience, all essential ingredients for emotional health and well-being. The staff who have delivered the group work programmes have reported the effectiveness of using this tool both in the sessions and in their other roles around the school as a way of managing behaviour. They have also noticed that their increased self-awareness has resulted in an improved understanding of children's behaviour. The concrete examples of reflective language and staff reflective practice provided enable school staff to become more aware of what, why and how children communicate through their behaviour along with increasing their awareness of how they respond to this. This change in staff thinking can result in a better understanding of themselves and why they react to certain situations, along with an increased awareness of other school staff. This improved working relationship may result in a positive impact on the children.

I invite all school staff regardless of their role to try the staff strategies and reflections, and explore using reflective language. This is a new way of behaving for school staff: experiment with it, use it tentatively using words such as wondering or perhaps or sometimes, rather than telling. While reading this book I encourage you to think about the children you work with on a daily basis and consider what they may be trying to communicate to you by their behaviour. Throughout the book I use 'can' or 'may' to reiterate the importance of remembering that all children are individuals and therefore may respond differently to situations.

I will refer to my own experiences of delivering the group work programmes along with the experiences of staff who have implemented them, as all of the group work activities have been delivered by me and teaching assistants, learning mentors and family workers. The staff delivering the group work felt it enhanced their understanding of children's behaviour and gave them an insight into what the children were trying to communicate. The other school staff including head teachers commented on the noticeable changes in the children after the intervention and felt that it helped them to be more integrated into school life. The group work is most effective when it is delivered as part of a whole school approach to emotional health and well-being.

The group work programmes in this book are tried and tested and have been successfully implemented by school staff in a variety of roles across several schools. They can be delivered easily throughout the school year and provide an ideal opportunity for more focused work for children who need extra support with their social and emotional development. The activities are devised as a six-week programme but can be adapted for use with individuals or pairs of children in a way that meets children's needs. The group work programmes provide an opportunity for children to practise and develop skills that increase the likelihood of them being socially included rather than excluded from school and society as a whole.

In order to protect the confidentiality of the children and staff, any case studies or examples are composite and names and details have been changed. They are drawn from a number of experiences from my work over several years.

I hope you will enjoy this book and the activities, and it will enable you to think differently about the children you work with.

Part One: Theory

A child-centred approach to emotional health and well-being and understanding children's behaviour

1 What does a child need to be emotionally healthy?

In order for children to achieve success at school they need a degree of healthy emotional and social development so that they are emotionally ready and able to learn. This involves being able to cope with success and failure and having the resilience to manage this, along with being able to ask for help when they need it. It includes having a sense of confidence and self-esteem, having self-reliance and independence appropriate to their age, having a positive self-image and a strong sense of self, along with being able to understand their own feelings and express them. They need the stability and security to be able to manage change and unpredictability without it eroding their feelings of safety. They also need to have the social skills to develop, build and sustain relationships with both adults and children. How many children are equipped with all these skills to be able to do this?

The experience of being emotionally healthy is achieved by a combination of all the above skills together and not in isolation, in the same way as a child's ability to hold a pencil is dependent on their hand–eye coordination and manipulative skills. It is the cumulative effect of the child's experiences, learned behaviours and reactions to events that help define their sense of self and their ability to deal with situations both in and out of school. Children need information and explanations about what is happening in order for them to be able to make sense of their experiences.

Self-regulation

In order for children to be able to regulate their own stress levels, they need to have had this experience from an adult. Babies are unable to regulate their own stress and they depend on their caregivers to regulate it for them. For example, when a baby cries because they are hungry, tired or upset and the adult responds with love and concern, this helps to reduce the baby's stress. If a crying baby is ignored or met with anxiety or hostility, it can increase their stress. The way the adult responds to this stress can either help the child to develop their own stress regulatory system, or create even more stress and prevent this development taking place. If the child gets what they need from an adult then a pattern develops that allows the child to begin to manage stress for themselves.

In order for children to develop healthily, adults need to respond to children's stress in a way that calms and soothes them rather than exacerbates their stress. For example, Tom, aged 3, is happily playing with a train when another child snatches it from him. Tom screams with rage and hits the child. If he is soothed, comforted, listened to and supported then this validates his feelings and enables stress regulatory systems to be developed. If he is offered a calm and clear explanation about not hitting other children then he is gradually able to understand that this behaviour is not acceptable. Tom is totally dependent on the stress regulating systems of a caring adult to help him to develop his own. If a caring adult is able to help him with his feelings and acknowledge and soothe his distress, he gradually develops the ability to do this for himself. As stressful situations occur in his life, he has the ability to manage them due to his initial experiences of stress being held and helped by a caring adult.

However, if the adult responds to the situation by shouting at him, dragging him away or smacking him for hitting the other child, Tom will feel even more stressed and anxious and will be unable to develop self-regulation. He does not learn how to manage stress and anxiety for himself; instead he learns to be wary and fearful of other people and finds it extremely difficult to share. He is overwhelmed by his feelings and unable to self-regulate.

Case study

Nyall, aged 8, had regular tantrums at school where he would hurl himself across the room, throw things and on occasion bite the other children. He couldn't accept that he had to share and would snatch to get what he wanted.

Possible reasons for Nyall's behaviour:

- His dad regularly hit his mum if he wasn't happy with the meal she had provided.
- His younger sister took his toys from him and he was told he was a 'cry baby' and shouted at if he got upset.

When children have not had the experience of self-regulation being provided by a parent, school staff can contribute to fulfilling this role.

Strategies to help children to self-regulate

- Respond to the intensity of what the child is feeling and reinforce this with the appropriate tone of voice and facial expression; for example, 'It made you furious that you couldn't be at the front of the line today.'
- Validate the child's experience – it is very real for them so ensure they feel you are taking it seriously; for example, 'When Sam called you stupid it must have really hurt.'
- Support the child by helping them to find alternative ways to express their feelings if appropriate; for example, 'It's never ok to hit people, Michael, we need to find other ways that you can have your feelings and not hurt anyone when you have them.'
- Offer a calm and reassuring approach so the child feels you are affirming them and accepting rather than dismissing their feelings; for example, 'It can be really difficult when you want to have the red pen and someone else is already using it.'

The above responses enable the child to feel connected to, understood and recognised for who they are and what they are feeling. It gives the message 'All feelings are ok and I can help you with them.' It helps them to make the link between feelings and words. It affirms the pain the child is feeling and helps them to understand it. This helps them to feel less overwhelmed and alone with the feelings and therefore less scared. This will support the child with developing self-regulation. When an adult intervenes and offers support, it can reduce the anxiety levels for children along with validating rather than invalidating their experiences and feelings.

Staff strategy – angry arrow

Figure 1.1 Angry arrow

Create a calm/angry board by attaching an arrow with a paper fastener to a numbered background so that the arrow can be rotated (see Figure 1.1).

The child uses an arrow to assess how angry they are and are then supported to use calming techniques such as take a deep breath and count from 10 backwards or take a deep breath in count 1 then breath out in count 2, etc. up to 10 or more. Check with the child where they are now on their angry arrow and explore what they think has helped them.

The role of the facilitator in the group work programmes enables the children in the group to practise self-regulation and provides an opportunity for the facilitator to transfer these new skills to their role across the school. This alternative way of responding to children's feelings and behaviour can be modelled across the school and empowers all staff to use a different approach.

Staff strategy – releasing feelings

If a child needs help to manage their feelings of anger and frustration, offer them a large scribble pad and pens or crayons for them to use when they need to. Ensure they are able to access this easily and offer support and demonstrations if needed.

This activity provides a powerful message that all feelings are acceptable and an alternative and constructive way of helping a child to release them. It can be a useful tool to assist them in the process of self-regulation.

Self-reliance

Case study

Hussein, aged 8, was getting changed for PE with the rest of his class. One of his trainers had a big knot in the lace which he kept tugging at and trying to undo. His class teacher approached him and offered to help him. He shook his head, not looking up and began to bite at the knot with his teeth. She explained that if he didn't hurry up the class would start the lesson without him and offered him help again. He shook his head again and started trying to shove his foot in the back of the trainer, causing him to wobble and fall over.

Possible reasons for Hussein's behaviour:

- As a baby if he cried no one came.
- When he fell and hurt himself no one comforted him.
- If he was hungry then he got himself some food even if this meant stealing it.

It was impossible for Hussein to ask for or allow himself to receive help as he'd learned to rely on the only person that had always been there for him, himself. He had learned to adopt self-reliance as a way of coping and feared neediness or asking for help as it had not been available for him. At school he presented as someone who was self-contained and could manage on his own. This resulted in him finding relationships with both children and adults challenging, as he was controlling and manipulative as a way of feeling safe in his world.

In order for children to develop a sense of independence and ability to depend on themselves it helps if they have had an experience of being able to depend on an adult who has responded appropriately to their needs. For a child who has not had this experience or it has been inconsistent, it can feel terrifying to both ask for help and be able to receive it. These children have learned to be overly reliant on themselves as a way of feeling safe and will need plenty of support to change this behaviour. They may think 'I can only rely on myself.' The challenge for these children is to trust that an adult will consistently support them and to understand that it is acceptable to ask for help from others.

Strategies for children who are overly reliant on themselves

- Understand that they have learned to do this as a way of feeling safe and ensure you do not take over or invade their space; for example, provide opportunities for them to work near you so they can access you easily and you can monitor whether they need help.
- Identify their need to do things for themselves and reflect on what it may feel like to change this; for example, 'I can see you are struggling to get that jigsaw piece in, I wonder what it would feel like if I helped you with it?'
- Let them lead their relationship with you and gradually access help in their own time and at their own pace by gentle reminders that you are available and willing to help them; for example, 'You are working very hard building that model; remember I can help you at any time if you need it.'
- Provide strong messages that validate it's ok to ask for help; for example, 'Even adults need help with things sometimes and it's ok to ask for what we need.'

The experience of developing self-reliance and becoming more independent is a gradual process that develops throughout childhood. In order for a child to achieve this in a healthy way it is necessary to provide them with opportunities to experience this. A child's ability to do things independently depends on several factors and is affected by their confidence and self-esteem along with the opportunity to develop these skills. In school there may be an expectation that children have a level of self-reliance that enables them to cope with the school day. For example, being able to change for PE with minimum or no help from adults, depending on their age. For a child who has no experience of this at home, perhaps because they are treated like a baby to meet their parent's needs, the very experience of this can be daunting.

Strategies to help children develop self-reliance

- Provide regular opportunities during the day for children to carry out tasks for themselves; for example, filling their own water bottle at the start of each day.
- Identify opportunities to help other children with small tasks; for example, 'Please could you help Nathan find his coat.'
- Ensure that children are rewarded for their efforts as well as their achievements; for example, 'You tried very hard to tie your shoe lace, well done.'
- Talk to the child's parents and identify something they have done well or achieved that day; encourage them to see the importance of the child having opportunities to do things for themselves at home.

Self-confidence and self-esteem

A child's sense of self-worth is deeply affected by their confidence and self-esteem. For children who have a poor sense of self, the school day can be made up of regular experiences that can erode this even further. However, there are also frequent opportunities to enhance this and ensure that it is developed to maximise the child's full potential. A child with confidence and self-esteem is keen to try new things, may offer to have a lead part in the class assembly and has the ability to develop and maintain good relationships with adults and children alike. They are able to express feelings such as excitement and fear with equal confidence. They have learned to trust the adults in their lives to care for and support them and therefore have the ability to do this for other people. They may believe they are essentially good and likeable and experience other people as the same.

However, some children's experiences have resulted in them having a very different sense of themselves. They experience the world as a frightening and unsafe place where it is better not to try new things in case you fail or make a mistake. They have discovered that some adults are unpredictable and that things change frequently and therefore nothing can be relied on. They have learned that feelings are to be feared and kept to yourself as they can overwhelm you and make things even more frightening. A child with low self-esteem who lacks confidence may present as being unsure of themselves at school. They may resist or find excuses not to try new things and may find it hard to express and manage their feelings. They may believe they are essentially bad and unlikeable and experience other people as better than them and more deserving.

Staff strategy – box of wishes

Teacher has a box of wishes on her table which are written by the class depending on their age or by school staff; e.g. wishing you a fun playtime.

At the start of each day a different child chooses one; work through the class register to ensure each child has a turn. The child returns the wish to the teacher at the end of the day and when the box is empty they are put back in the box and reused.

Strategies to develop confidence and self-esteem

- Provide opportunities to make choices wherever possible throughout the day, no matter how small; for example, writing with a pen or a pencil so they feel they have a voice and their opinions are important.
- Identify positive aspects of who they are and how they behave; for example, 'You were really kind when you held the door open for me.'
- Acknowledge and praise them for their achievements and successes no matter how small.
- Introduce emotional vocabulary to them; for example, 'It can make us feel proud when we do something well.'

There may also be children in school who appear to be overconfident and demand that they are chosen for everything, appear to know all the answers and may present as being happy in themselves. However, this may be a result of needing to be in control and manage situations around them in order to feel safe. This behaviour may be observed in children who have experienced domestic violence or other traumatic experiences and are desperately trying to establish some sense of security and stability in their lives. They may behave in ways that are challenging to school staff such as questioning them and trying to get them to make mistakes or get things wrong. This may be caused by their need to test adults in order to ascertain their reactions to events; for example, 'Miss Brogan always seems very calm, but I bet I can make her cross if I push her enough.'

This child may have learned to feel over-responsible for the adults in their lives and need to check out whether all adults are unpredictable. While this behaviour can be challenging to deal with at times, it can be useful to explore what may be going on for the child and how they may be feeling. It may be difficult for school staff to accept that children who present as controlling and challenging may actually be feeling frightened and vulnerable. However, if children feel that school staff are unable to manage them they may feel scared and this can reaffirm the negative feelings they already have about themselves.

Strategies for children who appear overconfident

- Remain in charge and be predictable wherever possible.
- Prepare them in advance for any changes that may occur in order to develop their ability to trust that adults mean what they say.
- Acknowledge and express emotional reactions to things; for example, 'Being in a different room can make us feel anxious as we are not used to it.' This may encourage them to begin to voice their own feelings in situations where they feel uncomfortable.

Self-image

Children who have a positive self-image are able to share their happiness about their appearance in a healthy way; for example, showing you their new shoes or haircut. This is an important aspect of children learning to be happy with who they are and along with self-confidence and self-esteem plays a role in self-acceptance. However, for some children this can be a preoccupation and override any sense of the person they are. They may feel that the person they are is defined by how they look and what they wear rather than the qualities and attributes they have. This needs to be handled in a sensitive way by focusing on their personal characteristics.

A child who has a poor self-image may put themselves down by criticising their appearance and making comments such as 'I hate my hair'. This may demonstrate a deeper sense of self-loathing and needs to be monitored closely. They may also have a lack of body awareness and disinterest in their appearance. This may be noticeable if a child has experienced neglect and may be unaware that their clothes or bodies are unclean. These children may be particularly vulnerable to being bullied by other children, especially as they start to become more aware of appearances as they get older. A balance between the two extremes is emotionally healthy, where a child is happy to get themselves and their clothes dirty playing outside but is also happy to wash their hands when they return to class.

Strategies to promote a positive self-image

- Monitor children who avoid messy activities and don't like getting dirty and encourage them to participate by providing aprons and acknowledging their anxieties; for example, 'You seem unsure about touching the clay, would it help if I broke a small piece off for you?'
- Ensure children have a healthy balance between focusing on their appearance and their qualities.
- Share positive comments about children's appearance where relevant and appropriate, without embarrassing them or excluding other children.

Self-belief

Children who have a strong self-belief are able to share their dreams and aspirations and have a sense of determination and perseverance that motivates them to do well. They are able to commit to achieving their goals and work towards them; for example, being captain of the football team or elected to the school council. These children appear to have a drive to do well and are intrinsically motivated to do this. This self-belief is initially developed through external mechanisms such as parental support and encouragement and rewards. However, over time it can be self-created and self-generated to ensure it continues to develop and grow.

Schools can play a crucial role in supporting children who have little or no self-belief, and while this is initially a slow process it is one that is achievable and can make a fundamental difference to children's lives. The development of self-belief initially starts within the family and for a child who lives with criticism, hostility and rejection it is an enormous task to alter what they have learned and experienced. A child's sense of self-worth can be activated by instilling a sense of them deserving to experience good things in their life; this is difficult but crucial for children who have experienced rejection or who have a sense of themselves as not being good enough. The work of school staff in achieving this is immense but achievable.

Strategies to develop self-belief

- Identify attributes you appreciate in children and share these with them, for example, 'I've noticed you really focus when we are doing circle time, I think you're a very good listener.'
- Acknowledge children's efforts and attempts at achieving things; for example, 'You tried hard to complete all your maths today, well done for working so well.'
- Introduce motivational vocabulary throughout the day; for example, 'I could see you were very determined when you were running the race today.'

Personal responsibility and self-awareness

An understanding of personal responsibility and self-awareness is necessary for a child to be able to change their behaviour. The combination of both of these enables a child to understand about important concepts such as differences of opinion and acceptance of other people. The ability to accept themselves and their own strengths and areas to work on enables children to develop this same acceptance of other people. This is linked closely with self-regulation, confidence and self-belief as they are all necessary ingredients for self-awareness and personal responsibility. An activity in the group work programme that focuses on acknowledging differences enables children to see the value in people being different and focuses on the positive side of this. In some families, difference may be seen as something negative and this provides an alternative way to view this.

Staff strategy – two sides to every story

Give two children a scenario of an argument to act out to the rest of the class. Ask the rest of the class to write down what they have just seen and then ask each person to read their version out to the class. How many versions were the same or even similar?

Use this activity to discuss how easy it is to have different versions of the same event. Ask the class to share their experiences of this happening and how it felt.

If a child has an understanding of personal responsibility they are able to acknowledge when they make mistakes and accept accountability for the choices they have made. They have a strong enough sense of themselves to be able to accept that getting things wrong is an important part of learning and to move on from this. They are aware that their behaviour has an impact on other people and are able to recognise when it may be appropriate to change this for other people's benefit.

When children have had no evidence of this experience operating within their family, it may be very difficult for them to grasp. The concepts of patience, acceptance and honesty can be difficult to understand and implement if this is not your experience outside school. It is important that we spend time explaining these ideas and their meaning to children, rather than assume they already have an understanding. The concept of patience can be linked to mistrust where having to wait for an outcome may be a frightening experience. The experience of this for some children may be too painful if, for example, your dad suddenly left home one night and you haven't seen or heard from him since and no one has explained to you what is happening or when or whether you will see him again. The feelings surrounding this experience may be reactivated whenever the child has to wait for a long time or be patient. If the adults in their family blame each other and other people when things go wrong or deny anything is their fault as 'things just happen', then it can be very confusing for children to understand the idea of actions having consequences and people having responsibility for the choices they make.

The role of school in providing opportunities for children to understand and gain positive experiences from these ideas is therefore crucial. The whole school ethos can be based around this and linked in to the behaviour and reward system. This is explored in more detail in Chapter Four.

Strategies to develop personal responsibility and self-awareness

- Discuss and celebrate uniqueness and differences between the children and staff in school so children value this as a positive experience.
- Provide opportunities to explore honesty, patience and acceptance so children understand these concepts; for example, 'Let's see how many times we can be patient today in class; I want you to help me find examples of when we are doing this.'
- Identify and praise children for their individual choices, especially if they are different to the other children; for example, 'I see you're the only one to have used the pink paint Matthew; well done for making the choice that you wanted.'

Resilience

The development of resilience can be viewed as one of the most vital ingredients for emotional health and well-being. The ability to deal with situations and bounce back after adversity is of paramount importance for all children, but especially those who live with uncertainty and disruption outside school. For children whose lives consist of them being criticised and ridiculed, or who live with drama and chaos, a sense of resilience is necessary for them to cope with this experience. The capacity for anyone to develop and sustain this is supported by the impact of other people who are able to encourage and believe in them.

In order to develop resilience, children need to experience some frustration to enable them to strengthen their ability to problem solve and learn. School staff can support this experience by ensuring they resist the urge to rescue or over help children. While children may not always be able to tolerate frustration, the opportunity to experience this while supported by a trusting adult is vital. The ability to practise having courage and facing fears can also contribute enormously to the development of resilience. A child who has experienced being brave and has had their experience validated by a caring adult is more able to strengthen these skills. Children who are resilient are able to develop strategies to support themselves when they experience difficult situations and therefore have their own bank of resources to use when life becomes challenging. Their experience of using a strategy that has worked for themselves enables them to use this again when they need to.

Strategies to develop resilience

- Do a strategies mind map with the class to identify what we can do when life is challenging; for example, school tests, falling out with friends, etc.
- Encourage the class to make their own courage creatures out of art materials. Keep these on display and integrate them into lessons and situations; for example, 'Today may be difficult as we've got our tests; you can choose to have them on your desk if you would like to.'
- Acknowledge situations where a child has faced their own challenge and discuss it with them, exploring the skills they feel they used; for example, 'You showed great strength when you walked away when Ryan was calling you names and found an adult to tell.'

It is essential that we consider not only how we can develop the resilience necessary for emotional health in children, but also have awareness of ensuring we do not destroy them. When a child's sense of self is fragile and gradually being developed by positive affirmations of who they are and what they do, we need to be aware of how easy it can be for this to disintegrate as a result of comments, looks, tone of voice, etc. While it is unrealistic and unhealthy to expect children to never be exposed to this, it is useful for school staff to develop a heightened awareness of this and to reflect on how their behaviour may be received by children. This is explored in more detail in Chapters Two and Five.

At school children are sent out to play at playtime with the assumption that they know what to do and how to do it. Some children have no idea where to start with this and either wander aimlessly round or stand in the corner or attempt to connect with other children and end up in trouble or fights. They do not have the skills or experience to be able to manage relationships with others. Relationship difficulties can flood over from break time to the classroom and interfere with learning. For children to manage school life and all the highs and lows that come with it they need to feel safe in themselves and safe in their world. School provides them with the opportunity to take risks, manage frustration, anxiety and disappointment, all terrifying experiences for children who have no resilience and no positive experience of this.

Inconsistencies

The experience of erratic and inconsistent parenting where children are provided with extremely rigid rules or no rules at all can make life very frightening and unsafe. For these children, the ability to control what they are able to in school by being manipulative and controlling of other people, including adults is a strategy they have developed to make themselves feel safe in an ever-changing and unpredictable world. For a child who goes home on Monday with paint on his jumper and Mum reacts by laughing, then on Tuesday Mum reacts by screaming, may internalise the message 'No matter what I do I can't get it right.' For these children life can feel full of despair and lacking in hope. This may result in them having extreme reactions to situations, e.g. sobbing and being distraught about a broken pencil. They may have no sense of responsibility and blame other people all the time. Their core belief about themselves may be 'I'm a bad person; I don't deserve to be liked or happy.' They lack confidence, have low self-esteem and poor social skills and may see themselves as worthless and have intense feelings of shame. They may actively set up situations that seek to confirm this distorted sense of themselves. They may refuse to participate as they feel 'What's the point?' and can come across as defiant, aggressive or lazy at school. A stable relationship with a member of school staff may enable them to feel supported and secure.

In families where children are given too much or too little responsibility they are either never able to be a child or never able to grow up. Children, who are given too much responsibility, perhaps by being expected to care for younger siblings, can present as overly responsible and bossy in school. They may also present as always being passive and behaving in a way that demonstrates that their needs aren't important; for example, letting other children go first all the time. The children who are overprotected and never given any responsibility may find it difficult to make choices as they may have little or no sense of who they are and what they like and dislike. Having either an over- or underprotective parent can be damaging to a child's sense of self and their self-esteem, along with their sense of feeling safe and secure. Children who experience intensely critical parenting by them insisting on perfection, teasing, ridiculing, humiliating the child or shaming or discounting them by name calling or ignoring them, may expect other adults in their lives to respond in the same way. At school these children may be constantly looking for evidence to affirm this negative sense of themselves as worthless.

Differences between home and school

In families where the acceptable way of communicating may be through anger and/or aggression, the social norms and expectations of school are very difficult for children to understand and follow. Children who live in constant fear and turmoil may find it difficult to relax and enjoy school as they are constantly on the lookout for potential danger from other children, adults or the environment, whether these are real or imagined. This constant state of hyper vigilance is very stressful and children in these situations may have learned that it is not safe to relax as they need to be constantly alert for danger. This has a detrimental effect on their attention and concentration, as well as impairing their social and emotional development.

If children grow up in families where there is often an abundance of drama and lots of stress and excitement around it, they may bring that experience in to school and always be in the middle of every situation, telling long, dramatic and sometimes difficult to follow accounts of other people's behaviour. They may display lots of 'notice me' behaviours such as calling out, sighing, saying they are hurt or unwell and playing the role of victim and 'poor me' extremely well. For these children, it is very difficult to manage the day-to-day life of school without the adrenalin rush of drama and excitement that they are used to, and they may seek to create it for themselves.

The written and unwritten codes of behaviour expected in school can be opposite to the expectations outside school for some children, resulting in confusion and poor conscience development.

Case study

Jenny, aged 10, would constantly lie, sometimes steal from the other children and adamantly deny her behaviour even if she was caught by school staff.

Possible reasons for Jenny's behaviour:

- She had learned at an early age that it was not acceptable to make mistakes and that it was better to lie than tell the truth.
- If she dropped or spilled something at home she was ridiculed and criticised.
- Her older brothers regularly took money from her mum's purse.
- She had been shopping with her mum when she stole food from the supermarket and had learned that if you didn't have enough money then it was acceptable to take something that wasn't yours.

For children to feel safe, stable and secure, it helps if they have had an experience of feeling this, along with a safe and consistent relationship with an adult. For some children inconsistency and unpredictability are the norm and are familiar to them. They may have experienced parents who, although they are physically present, are emotionally absent and preoccupied with their own needs and therefore unaware of the needs of their child or unable to respond to them. These children can find school life extremely challenging where they are unable to hide in the shadows and are brought into the spotlight by their behaviour.

Providing new experiences

In order to change these children's destructive view of themselves, they need plenty of new experiences where the adults are able to affirm their efforts at tasks, even if they don't succeed or complete them, and to be provided with meaningful praise and encouragement. They may be preoccupied with the adult relationships at school and may struggle to focus on tasks and hear instructions. The group work programmes provide the opportunity of being in a small group with a familiar and consistent adult, at the same time and in the same place each week. This experience provides children with an opportunity to experience consistency and predictability. The emotional focus of the group provides children with the opportunity to have their feelings acknowledged and validated rather than ignored or dismissed. If children are not able to express their feelings when they occur, the experience may stay in their body resulting in them feeling stressed, anxious and scared. The opportunity to practise expressing feelings within the group work sessions increases their ability to continue this outside the sessions.

The group work programmes have been designed to develop children's emotional health and well-being along with providing them with essential skills for everyday life as shown in Table 1.1. The facilitator's guidelines to accompany each session focus on identifying, acknowledging and reflecting possible feelings, along with recognising possible difficulties, and praising and encouraging the children for their contributions. This approach enables the children to make links between their feelings and behaviour and experiment with different behaviours in a safe and supportive environment.

Table 1.1 How group work promotes emotional health and well-being

Experience in the group	Potential impact on the child
Children are praised and encouraged	Builds self-esteem
Opportunities to practise and develop new skills	Develops independence and self-reliance
Identifies children's individual qualities	Promotes a positive self-image
Focuses on respecting and exploring differences	Teaches acceptance of self and others
Identifies and acknowledges feelings	Increases emotional vocabulary
Provides permission to get things wrong and make mistakes	Promotes self-acceptance and builds resilience
Celebrates individuality	Develops a sense of self
Identifies and acknowledges effort	Develops a sense of trust
Encourages a commitment to completing tasks	Promotes personal and group responsibility
Encourages children to take risks	Develops self-belief

Children who are emotionally healthy have the skills and ability to tolerate frustration and uncertainty and have a strong sense of themselves as valuable individuals. They are able to relate to others with the skills and confidence to build and develop positive relationships, and have the ability to treat themselves and others with value and respect. They have the skills and resilience to cope with life's disappointments and are able to appreciate and enjoy their own and other people's successes. The group work programmes provide an opportunity for children to practise and develop these skills which are then transferable outside the group sessions into the rest of their school life, making the effects of the sessions long lasting.

2 The impact of external circumstances on a child's ability to learn and succeed at school

By the time children start school they have already received strong messages about themselves, other people and the world. They form their initial sense of themselves and how they are perceived as people from within the family, and this can be either positive or negative. A child's internal rule book is developed early, along with their template of how to build and manage relationships. The family models ways of managing feelings that provide children with experiences that they bring to school and use in their daily life. All of this occurs within the family, which can be seen as the child's first classroom. The more information that school staff are provided about a child's background and experiences (while maintaining any necessary confidentiality issues), the better equipped they are to respond to the child's needs.

Physical well-being

There are some children who have many barriers that can prevent them accessing their learning and reaching their potential. If a child's basic needs for food, appropriate clothing and sufficient sleep are not being met they are disadvantaged before they have entered the school building to start their day (see Table 2.1).

Table 2.1 Potential barriers to learning

Situation	Child is preoccupied with	Impacts on learning
Wearing sandals in winter	Feeling cold	Can't concentrate, shivers, rubs feet
Falling asleep on sofa very late at night	Feeling tired	Yawns, can't engage or retain information, poor concentration, lack of coordination, listless, lethargic, fidgety, no resilience, gets upset easily
Missing breakfast and other meals	Feeling hungry, thinking about lunchtime and food	Anxious about the time, fixated with the clock, obsessed with food

Do my needs matter?

All human beings have basic emotional needs for love, validation, acknowledgement and understanding. Within the family a child receives messages about the importance of their needs, and accumulates experiences of how these are responded to. If their needs are responded to consistently by a loving, caring adult who tries to meet them on a regular basis, the child internalises a strong and positive sense of themselves as a worthwhile person whose needs are important and do matter. However, if a child is frequently ignored or met with hostility and resistance when they express their needs, they learn that they are not important or worthwhile and their needs do not matter (see Table 2.2). A child with this experience may conclude that other people's needs are more important than theirs and will put other people first and try and meet their needs. For example, a child in school with a bag of sweets who gives them all away to the other children, without having any themselves. If children receive messages 'Don't want, don't need, don't expect, don't say much', it is extremely difficult for them to have a positive sense of themselves as a worthwhile person.

Table 2.2 Impact of parent behaviour on child

Parent behaviour	Child learns
Mum is always busy	I must not disturb her
Dad is often out with his friends and doesn't spend time with me	I am not interesting, Dad doesn't like me
Mum frequently shouts and is angry	I must not ask for things or make a fuss
Dad is always bad tempered and unhappy	I must be cheerful and try to make Dad happy
Both parents ignore the child	I am not important or worthwhile
Mum criticises the child on a regular basis	I am a bad person and unlovable

Children who live with these experiences constantly occurring can develop coping strategies as a way of surviving in the world. These may manifest in school by them being controlling, bossy and manipulative, as well as trying to please other people. When a child tries to control the class and challenges adults on a regular basis, they may present as having no fear and not being bothered, but they have developed this behaviour as a way of feeling safe in a world that often feels very unsafe. They may use this coping strategy as a way of managing their feelings; for example 'If I pretend I don't care then I won't feel hurt or upset.'

Case study

Alex, aged 8, would often contribute random and unrelated comments at inappropriate times during the school day. During a literacy lesson he put his hand up to answer a question and said, 'Miss, cats like sleeping by the fire.' The class responded by laughing and Alex looked hurt and confused. His parents had recently separated and he was worried about when he would be seeing his dad again as he had overhead a phone argument last night with his mum telling his dad he couldn't see Alex until he gave her some money. His random answer was because he was thinking about his dad and had remembered his dad's cat liked sleeping by the fire.

I suggested his teacher offer to spend five minutes with him every lunchtime where he could share his news and that he could try and hold on to his news during lesson times. This enabled Alex to feel validated rather than dismissed and helped him to engage more fully with his learning during the lessons. It also provided the message to Alex that his thoughts and feelings were important.

It's all my fault

Some children may experience themselves as undeserving and may feel overly responsible for things. This may be due to them operating socially and emotionally at a much younger level of development than their chronological age. They may learn that no matter what they do or how they do it, they are wrong. This can result in them internalising the belief that everything is their fault and they are wrong because they are a bad person. Consequently they may have thoughts such as:

- 'I am so bad I make Mum angry all the time.'
- 'I gave my teacher a sore throat because he shouted at me yesterday.'
- 'If I had eaten all my dinner Dad wouldn't have hit Mum.'
- 'If hadn't lost my coat then Mum wouldn't be crying.'

These children live with the contradiction that they can feel both powerful and powerless. They may present in school as being hyper vigilant, noticing everything and being overly concerned with what is happening around them as a way of trying to manage their feelings of anxiety and fear.

Internal belief system

Children develop an internal belief system about themselves by the messages they receive from other people. These messages define whether they are lovable, valuable and worth listening to and spending time with, and have a significant influence on a child's confidence, self-esteem, self-belief and how they feel about themselves (see Table 2.3).

Table 2.3 Developing a positive internal belief system

Parent behaviour	Child feels and internalises the message
Helps child with homework	I am worth helping and I feel good about myself
Attends parents evening	Mum is interested in me and how I am doing at school
Praises child	I am a good person and I can do useful things
Asks child about their day	How I feel is important and I am worth getting to know
Helps child to manage conflict with sibling	Adults can help me

Dealing with contradictions

The family is the place where children learn an initial code of conduct with guidelines, rules and expectations for behaviour. This code of conduct may be in conflict with the behavioural expectations of the school, resulting in the child having to navigate their way through a whole new set of rules. The dilemma for the child may be, 'Do I please my parents or my teacher?' Either way this may mean going against or gaining disapproval from one of the significant adults in the child's life. This is particularly difficult for a child who is constantly trying to get it right and please other people as they are stuck in a no-win situation.

The conflict between the different codes of conduct at home and at school may cause particular problems after school holidays, where the family will have had a much stronger influence over the child due to the length of time spent with them. The more differences there are between home and school in terms of expectations and behaviour, the longer and more difficult it may be for the child to adjust to the return to school.

Staff strategy – to help a child adjust to the return to school after the holiday

Explore their behaviour chart with a significant adult as soon as they return to school, ensuring they understand it.

Take them for a walk around school to remind them of the behavioural expectations of school.

This strategy can help a child to make the adjustment to being back at school more easily and increases the likelihood of them coping better with the transition (see Table 2.4).

Table 2.4 Conflicting messages between home and school

Child's behaviour	Response at home	Response at school
Persistently challenging adults	Adult gives child what they want	Child is reprimanded and kept in at playtime
Has a tantrum	Adult ignores them	Child receives explanation about how to behave
Hits another child	Adult hits them	Child gets age-appropriate consequence
Swears	Adult laughs	Child gets name on the board in class
Tries to manipulate and control adult	Adult gives in to child's demands	Child is talked to by teacher who explains about behaviour expectations at school
Interrupting adults	Adult talks louder or shouts	Child is reprimanded and reminded of school rules

If there are no rules or boundaries at home for the child's behaviour, or these are inconsistent and changeable, depending on how the parent feels at the time; the child will learn that life can be unpredictable and that adults can be manipulated and controlled at times. For these children, the world can be a very confusing and unsafe place as the code of conduct at home and school is incompatible. If a child has learned at home that if you challenge adults, plead for your own way and sulk if you don't get it, and adults give in to you, they will try this approach at school, with a very different result for their behaviour.

Child learns

- I can talk back to adults.
- I can do what I want when I want.
- I can manipulate adults to get my own way.
- I can shout when I want something.
- I interrupt adults to get myself heard.
- I can ignore adults when I choose to.

If a child tries behaviour at school that produces a different outcome at home, it can be very upsetting and confusing for them if it doesn't achieve their desired result. Children who use manipulative, challenging and controlling behaviour at school may have learned to do this as a way of trying to create their own consistency in an inconsistent world. They are attempting to reproduce an experience that is familiar to them as a way of feeling safe. For example, a child who argues relentlessly that they should be allowed to do PE in their shoes rather than their trainers may have learned that not only do adults give in eventually, but also 'I am used to being in charge and will do all I can to ensure that it stays that way.'

Children who may have no rules or consequences for their behaviour at home and have lots of freedom may experience school as very restrictive. These children can live in a constant state of high anxiety and it may be difficult for them to manage even very small changes at school. They may constantly oppose authority and struggle to accept inconsistencies happening at school; for example, becoming very upset that you are not using the hall for games and saying 'But you said we were going in the hall, Miss'. It is crucial that children who experience these difficulties are provided with a sense of predictability and routine and offered explanations as much as possible, in order to reduce their need to try and create this for themselves, and allow them to feel safe and settled in school. However, families who use corporal punishment at home as a way of managing their child's behaviour may feel that the school is too soft and that this has a negative impact on the child's behaviour at school. Equally, the school may feel that the parents approach is too harsh. The result is confusion and anxiety for the child who is caught between the two conflicting approaches.

Staff strategy – a child's day

Provide a visual timetable for the child on a daily basis with a timeline of events (written or pictures depending on the child's needs). Include changes of staff and room if applicable. Go through it with them at the start of each day and check they have understood it, encouraging them to explore any uncertainties. Ensure the child can access it easily throughout the day.

When a child receives attention for negative behaviour, rather than positive, they may view themselves as negative. If a child doesn't get a response from an adult at home when they show or tell them something positive, it can reinforce the message that 'good' behaviour doesn't get a response but 'bad' behaviour does. This can result in the child feeling they need to display negative behaviour to be noticed and get adult attention. If they only receive attention for negative behaviour at home, while at school they receive attention for positive behaviour, they may not understand why the focus is different. A child that is noticed for their 'bad' behaviour rather than their 'good' may conclude that they are bad rather than good. It may reinforce the message that nothing about them is good. The contradictive response they receive at school may confuse them further, 'Am I bad or good? Dad thinks it's funny when I swear, but it makes Mrs Thompson very cross.' It can be an arduous task for schools to undo the early and external messages that children receive about themselves, and while they may be unable to do much to change the child's external world, they are able to change their internal world by providing them with an alternative image of themselves as a good person.

Getting it wrong

The responses that children absorb from home about making mistakes can have a huge influence on their school life on a daily basis. It can impact on a child's ability to try something new, to persevere with something they find difficult and to be honest about getting something wrong. When a child cheats on a test either by copying another child or changing an answer when marking it themselves, this behaviour may indicate a very fragile sense of themselves, rather than a manipulative controller which is how they may be perceived. A child that has learned that it is not safe enough to tell the truth may be so adamant and highly skilled at lying that the member of staff starts to doubt themselves. For this child, the feelings of shame may be overwhelming and need to be avoided at all costs, hence the lying and determination not to be found out.

Case study

Kyra, aged 9, came from a family where the adults lied to each other, denied their own behaviours by blaming other people and used aggression as a way of getting other people to do as they wanted. Kyra learned at a very young age that it was not ok to make mistakes, when she accidentally knocked a cup of juice over when she was three and was beaten and sent to bed without her tea. At school she was terrified of getting things wrong but had learned to hide behind bravado and pretending she wasn't bothered as a way of dealing with the overwhelming feelings she had if she failed something. When she snapped a pencil she had been tapping on a desk in front of her class teacher, she immediately denied it and started arguing with the teacher. She was so convincing in her justification and explained that 'it was already broken' that her teacher started to doubt herself and what she had seen. The other children in the class, however, had seen her do it and this reassured her.

For Kyra, facing the consequences of what she had done to the pencil was so frightening that she was determined to convince her teacher that she hadn't done it. She had learned that it is not ok to make mistakes and, when you do, terrifying things happen. She had also learned that it is not safe to admit to what you have done and she did not trust that her teacher would not have an extreme reaction to what had happened.

Kyra needs:

- opportunities to experience losing and getting things wrong with an adult on an individual basis who can acknowledge her feelings, e.g. 'It can feel awful when you get something wrong, but everyone gets things wrong sometimes';
- adults to acknowledge their own mistakes to her, e.g. 'I snapped my shoe laces this morning when I was putting my shoes on, but it's ok because accidents happen and I can buy new laces';
- validation of her feelings, e.g. 'It can be really frightening to tell the truth as you don't know what I might say or do';
- adults to respond to her attempts to try new things in a positive and reassuring way, e.g. 'You've been very brave trying your new reading book that can feel like a scary thing to do';
- positive responses to her making mistakes, e.g. 'You tried really hard to do those sums even though they were very hard for you, it's ok to get things wrong, well done for trying.'

When a child behaves in this way it can have a big impact on their learning and ability to make and sustain friendships with other children. If a child is scared of trying things for fear of getting it wrong they may be disruptive, disengaged and tell lies. They may also sabotage the situation; for example, being rude and aggressive to the teacher the morning of a school trip so they are not allowed to go. The child may have learned that feelings of disappointment are easier to manage than the fear of new experiences. Children who sabotage things may believe 'Good things can't happen to me, I don't deserve to have nice things happening.'

Learning how to manage feelings

The reactions to feelings and how they are acknowledged and expressed within the family provide children with a template that they may replicate at school. As discussed in Chapter One, self-regulation and the ability to identify and respond to feelings is learned in childhood and carried on into adulthood. Children learn self-regulation by having an adult who can help them to identify, name and express their feelings. Children learn this at a very young age as baby's brains are still developing and are very sensitive to stress and unable to regulate their own stress and depend on their carers to regulate it for them. The way that adults respond to this stress can either soothe and alleviate it or exacerbate it. If they are responded to in a way that soothes it, they gradually develop their own stress management system. If they receive what they need, they become able to manage the stress more easily themselves. However, if the adult responds in a way that increases the stress, it can heighten the anxiety levels and prevent this development taking place. Children who do not receive soothing from an adult in times of distress and upset do not develop their own stress regulating system, unless another significant adult takes on these vital parental functions with the child on a regular basis. School staff can play a vital role in helping children learn to understand and express their feelings and therefore develop self-regulation.

If a child has not learned self-regulation, it can have an enormous impact on their learning and relationships at school. They may become involved in arguments and fights with other children and may be unable to accept or deal with the feelings evoked by this. This can also affect their ability to focus and engage with their learning as they may be preoccupied with trying to manage their feelings. Their inability to self-regulate may affect their friendships with other children and relationships with school staff. It may also be more difficult for them to be involved in extra curricular activities such as sports club due to their difficulties managing competition and failure.

The way that the adults in the child's family respond to and demonstrate managing their own feelings impacts on how children learn to do this and the messages they receive about how acceptable this is. This may also be in conflict with school and the messages they receive there. For example, how do the child's parents express anger and frustration (see Table 2.5)?

Table 2.5 Expressing feelings in the family

Situation	Feeling	Expressed by parent
Post office is closed	Anger	Punches the wall outside the shop
Can't open a jar	Frustration	Throws it across the room
Has an argument with a friend	Sadness	Gets drunk
Will be late for an appointment	Anxiety	Shouts and screams at the bus driver

All the above situations are terrifying for children who may learn that feelings are not good things to have and should be avoided. When children express their feelings in ways that contradict the norms of behaviour at home, this may result in them experiencing being humiliated, shamed and ridiculed. For example, a 10-year-old boy who cries may experience teasing from family members and internalise strong messages about this such as 'I need to be strong and not show my feelings, crying is a sign of weakness and failure.' When children learn to hold on to their feelings and not express them it can be very difficult for them to change this behaviour. They may develop a 'don't care' attitude to learning, friendships and school which can be a learned response to avoiding having to deal with feelings.

Within the family children witness reactions to everyday events, and these may affect their responses to drama and excitement. If a child experiences excitement, drama and attention from everyday events involving relationships and conflict, they learn that drama is important and this is how to get a response from the adults around them. They may start to recreate this in school as it is familiar and they may crave the adrenalin and excitement that dramatic events can provide. For example, a child may return to class after playtime with a long and complicated story that involves lots of people and events. The teacher may not react in the way the child is expecting and therefore the child doesn't get the response they were looking for. The child may then proceed to create more drama by being disruptive and interrupting the lesson to get the attention they are craving. They may become overly involved in what other people are doing and provide commentaries on it. They may find it hard to just stick to the facts in events and not add their own fabrication which they think may result in them getting more attention.

Case study

Tara, aged 9, came from a large and prominent family in her local community. Both her parents had regular conflict with the neighbours, local families and other parents at the school. They were both frequent visitors to the school where they would challenge staff and demand an immediate meeting with the head teacher. After most lunchtimes Tara would have a story she urgently had to share with her teacher. They always involved several people, including lunchtime organisers and a series of events that were sometimes hard to follow. The class teacher was often amazed at how much could happen in a single lunchtime.

Tara needs:

- opportunities to develop confidence and feel good about herself without the need to create drama;
- a special job that can make her feel valued and enable her to contribute to the class, such as looking after the book corner;
- an adult to spend time with her helping her understand alternative ways of managing conflicts and building relationships.

Parental expectations

Parents will bring their own experiences of schooling and their attitude towards education and learning with them in to school. It is essential that school staff are aware of this and the potential impact it can have on the parent's ability to fully engage with and support their child's learning. If a child's parents have negative experiences of school and staff from their own childhood then it can take a great deal of courage to even walk through the school gates, let alone speak to teachers or approach the head teacher. If a child's parents are consistently avoiding entering the school it can be useful to explore the possible reasons for this and offer alternate times to talk to them if possible. There may be numerous reasons for this; for example, they may feel overwhelmed by the other parents, particularly if they experience them as loud and domineering.

Reflect: How do you experience parents?

Think about how you experience parents who are challenging or may be experiencing difficulties with school and ask yourself if you would be happy to wait around in the playground talking to them?

Some parents may believe that school is a waste of time and that children don't learn anything. They may think that school staff are too strict or too soft and say things like 'it never did me any good'. They may keep their children off school, not wake them up in the morning so the children are late, discourage them from doing homework, refuse to pay for school trips and never send the child's PE kit in. These parents are more difficult to engage with the school and their child's learning and may require additional support from a family worker or attendance officer if they are available through the school.

Case study

Emma was the parent of three children and had found her own school days to be very difficult as she was extremely shy and had been bullied by a large group of girls for many years. She had experienced the school staff as only being interested in the bright and lively pupils and after eventually finding the courage to tell one of them about being bullied, was dismissed as wasting the teacher's time. Emma then played truant regularly and stopped going altogether on her sixteenth birthday. She had left school with no qualifications and wanted her own children to do well at school. She was mistrustful of all school staff and appeared aggressive and volatile at times. She would rush in, shout at the children to hurry up and then chase them out of the school building. The school staff thought she was rude and disinterested in her children's education, and were amazed that the children all produced their homework on time and had their reading records signed every night.

The parent's relationship with their child

A useful indicator of both a parent's relationship with school and their child is how they meet and greet each other at the start and end of the school day. Does the child bring themselves and their siblings in to school alone, sometimes arriving too late or too early? Or are they brought to school by mum or dad who kisses them and tells them to have a good day. This start of the school day can impact enormously on the child's ability to settle in to class easily and engage with their learning. How are they greeted if they are collected by the parent at the end of the day; are they acknowledged or met with scowls and reprimands such as 'What's that on your jumper?' If the child shows the parent a certificate or picture they have made, does the parent respond or just carry on talking to another parent or continue their conversation on their mobile phone? All these responses provide children with messages about how loved, valued and important they are.

If a parent is critical and judgemental towards their child, the child learns 'I am not good enough, I can't get it right, it's not ok to be me, and there must be something wrong with me.' These can all have a strong impact on their self-esteem and self-worth and over time may gradually erode their sense of self. If a child feels unloved and unlovable as a result of the messages they receive they may seek external gratification through food, bullying others, and being demanding and clingy to school staff as a way to manage their feelings. This can all have a significant impact on the child's behaviour (see Table 2.6).

Table 2.6 Development of internal belief system

Child feels	Child learns	Child behaves
I'm not good enough	I am worthless	Tries to make other people happy
I can't get it right	I need to try harder	Tries to be perfect
It's not ok to make mistakes	I need to be perfect	Is bossy, manipulative, controlling
It's not ok to be me	I need to be different/someone else	Is always putting other people's needs before their own

Additional pressures on parents

The external difficulties that some parents may be dealing with on a daily basis may result in them not being able to meet the emotional needs of their children, however much they may want to. The impact of situations such as domestic violence, poverty, bereavement, poor housing, and drug and alcohol dependency may all result in a parent being stressed, anxious and preoccupied with their own problems. This may mean they are physically and/or emotionally unavailable for the child and may find it difficult to engage with the child's emotional needs. When a parent is stressed they may have no capacity to understand or meet the child's feelings as they can be too overwhelmed by their own. The parent may want to be able to do this for their child, but their own practical and emotional difficulties may be barriers to them being able to. Unfortunately, when children are living in circumstances like this, they can respond to the anxiety and stress by becoming more insecure and anxious themselves, creating another stress for the parent to manage.

Case study

Margaret had five children and was frequently complaining about the school and the way her children were treated. The school staff found her challenging and would turn round and start walking the other way if they saw her on the corridor, rather than face the torrent of negativity she sometimes had waiting for them. Since her youngest child had started full time at the school nursery, Margaret had found her days long and empty. She was at her happiest during the school holidays or if one of the children was unwell and had to stay at home with her.

The head teacher approached Margaret and asked her whether she would be willing to help organise and repair books in the school library with another parent as the school staff were struggling to find the time to do this. Margaret resisted at first but eventually agreed to 'give it a go'. The role created for her by the head teacher made her feel important, valued and that she had a purpose. She became more positive towards the school, seemed happier in herself and eventually started working as a lunchtime organiser.

The opportunity provided by this school enabled Margaret to realise she had something to offer and was able to contribute and receive attention in a positive way. It also enabled her to use her skills as a parent to find work.

The impact on children

When a child is living in a stressful situation such as domestic violence, their home can become a terrifying and unpredictable place, rather than a haven of security. The significant impact on children of living in these circumstances and the enormity of the problem can be hard to comprehend. A child may be preoccupied with what is happening at home and unable to engage with their learning. They may have difficulty retaining information and appear to be in their own world a lot of the time. If children live with fear it may affect their ability to hear instructions; for example, a child going to their drawer and just standing staring into space as they are unable to remember what they needed to do. Some children may pretend they are unwell and need to be sent home as a way of trying to check what is going on or staying at home to stop it happening. A child may deliberately forget his PE kit so the school will phone Mum to bring it in as a way of checking that she is safe.

Some children may have negative associations of mealtimes as this may be when the violence occurs, and they may either eat very fast to get away from the situation or pretend they are not hungry. They may have learned to accept feeling hungry as mealtimes at home are often disrupted due to fights and violence. A child who has experienced domestic violence may also come across as being very vigilant as they may have learned to be watchful as a way of trying to stay safe. Living with domestic violence may result in some children finding it difficult to make friends and manage relationships, due to confusion over what is acceptable and unacceptable behaviour. They may become quiet and withdrawn or become loud and fidgety with poor concentration. They may feel angry, confused, anxious, insecure and frightened. This may result in them having nightmares, being more tired than usual due to disturbed or lack of sleep.

Children who grow up in a family where there is domestic violence may learn powerful lessons about the use of control, intimidation and force in relationships. They can learn that aggression is part of everyday life and it is acceptable to shout at and hit other people. This can make it very confusing and difficult when they are at school where this behaviour is not seen as acceptable. They may try to placate school staff as they have learned to try and please other people as a way of trying to control the situation. Children who live with domestic violence may not experience positive relationships being modelled as they may have one parent who is the controlling aggressor and the other parent who is the terrified victim. This may make it hard for either parent to be consistently physically or emotionally available for the child, resulting in the family being a very frightening place at times.

Responsibility

Some children may have responsibilities for younger siblings, themselves and their parents, as a result of the adults in the family being unable to fulfil this caring role.

A child may take on a caring role for younger siblings which can involve getting them ready for school, making breakfast, bringing them to and from school and taking on the parenting role within the family. For example, a 7-year-old who goes on his bike to the corner shop at 7.30 am to buy bread so all the children can have toast before they go to school. Children may be involved in the financial concerns of the family and be aware of money worries which in turn become their worries. For example, an 8-year-old boy told me 'We've not got any money till Thursday so we're just having toast for our tea.' This knowledge of his family's money concerns created huge anxiety for this child, and he was often preoccupied (possibly with hunger), and anxious to please other people and therefore unable to fully engage with his learning.

Multiple transitions

For most children, managing daily school life with its challenges and changes along with moving to a new class at the end of each school year is enough to deal with. There are some children who along with this also move schools frequently for a multitude of reasons, including parents moving house, either through choice or necessity due to being rehoused. For these children the difficulties of dealing with school life on a daily basis are compounded. They may have had to move away from other family members and the community they are familiar with and start again on a regular basis. I have worked with a child who had moved from one school to another and back to the original school and then moved again, all within the space of less than two years. For this child, her ability to settle at school, manage the daily routine and build and maintain friendships became impossible. She was living with high levels of anxiety and was scared and confused, especially as her actual leaving day kept being changed.

Staff strategy – transition activity to help a child adjust to their new school

Story – Ask the child to create a story using words and pictures; e.g. This is Fred (draw a stick man), this is his new school (draw a building). I wonder how Fred might be feeling (angry/ scared/excited). I wonder what he might do. This is Fred's new teacher, etc.

When children live with this uncertainty and lack of consistence and security, it can be difficult for school to be the secure base it needs to be. The varied approaches that the different schools may have can result in the child feeling overwhelmed, unable to access learning and falling further behind with each change of school. This can impact on their confidence and self-esteem along with their ability to build and sustain friendships. This may result in them being more vulnerable to being bullied or becoming bullies themselves as a way of feeling more powerful in response to a situation that often renders them powerless. They may position themselves on the margins of school life as they are unsure how long they will be staying at a school and therefore can resist efforts made by school staff to help them settle. This is discussed in more detail in Chapter Five.

Staff strategy – helping a child settle

Identify a key person to be allocated to any new child to help them settle in to the class and the school. Make a welcome book for them with photos of them around the school with situations chosen by them. Allow them as much choice as possible and allow them to build relationships with adults and staff gradually, in their own time and at their own pace.

The wider community

Just as there can be differences between the code of conduct at home and at school, this can be reinforced by the wider community that children are living in (see Figure 2.1). There can be hierarchies of power between families and this experience may result in people living in fear. For example, an adult being scared to report the domestic violence they hear from their neighbours every night for fear of reprisals. There may be a different moral code that children are dealing with that may conflict with school; for example, a child who is asked not to lie, cheat or steal at school, but knows that their mum puts nappies under the bottom of the pushchair and walks out of the shop without paying for them. This child can be in conflict about what is right and wrong and may be unclear about how to get it right themselves. Is it ok to steal food if you are hungry or take nappies if you haven't got any money?

Schools face an enormous task of trying to change some of the behaviours that are aspired to and validated by the wider community in some areas. The way in which status and power is achieved and recognised in some communities may be very different to the experience that schools are trying to encourage children to develop. Is it good to be clever or do you have to be naughty to be noticed? It is a complex task to try and understand the impact this can have on children in terms of who they are and the expectations and code of conduct from the community versus school. There are different gender pressures on girls and boys and these can be in conflict with who the child is and the strengths and abilities the school is actively encouraging the child to pursue. For example, a boy who excels at singing or dance may not be encouraged by his family or the community to pursue this talent. The child can be caught in conflict of trying to gain approval from three external areas.

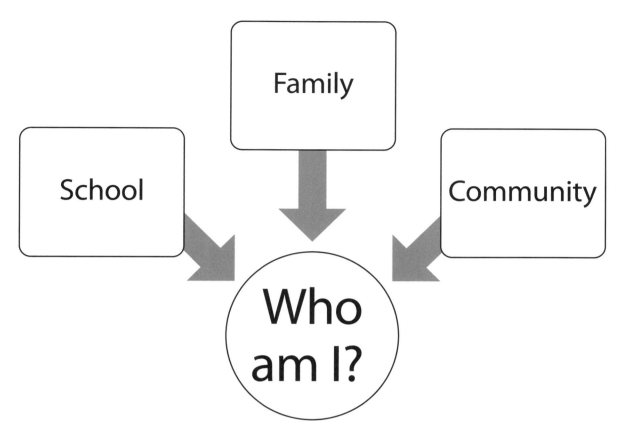

Figure 2.1 Who am I?

Some schools are operating in communities where there may be three or more generations of the same family living there who have never worked. The children in the family may never have known a family member who has worked. This can be in direct contrast to the messages of the school about working hard; how do we encourage children to integrate this message without saying that school is right and their family is wrong?

It can be very hard to develop aspirations, determination and motivation to succeed, along with a sense of purpose and having goals for children who may have only experienced the opposite outside school. It can be difficult to inspire children to be the best they can be and reach their full potential when it may conflict so strongly with the messages of their family and wider community. It is our responsibility to help generations of families to break this cycle.

3 What is this child trying to tell me?

Every child wants to be seen, known, valued and understood, but sadly for some children their behaviour can result in them getting the opposite of what they need. If a child is being disruptive, picking fights, being uncooperative and challenging school staff, or if a child is constantly trying to please other people, they are very clearly trying to communicate something to the adults around them. Most adults use language to express their needs and how they feel to other people. Most children, however, do not have the same language skills as adults and use behaviour to communicate their feelings. They need help from sensitive adults to help them work out and express what they feel. Every behaviour is trying to tell us something; for example, a tantrum may be communicating fear, frustration, boredom or anger. A child who is disruptive and challenging to school staff may be ensuring that he gets noticed and is not forgotten about or overlooked. It is the adults' role to try and understand what the child may be trying to tell them and then to respond accordingly.

How adults and children communicate

Reflect: Compare the two scenarios

Scenario 1

You are a class teacher for Year 3 and you had an argument with your partner before you left for work this morning, resulting in you arriving at school late and unprepared.

- How easy would you find it to settle at work and perform well?
- What would you be thinking and feeling?
- What could you do about this?
- How could you communicate your feelings and get support?

Scenario 2

You are 7 years old and you had an argument with your mum before you left for school this morning, resulting in you arriving late to school without your homework.

- How easy would you find it to settle in to class and engage with your learning?
- What would you be thinking and feeling?
- What could you do about this?
- How could you communicate your feelings and get support?

Sometimes as adults we can forget that we have the benefit of experience, developed language skills and the ability to articulate our thoughts and feelings if we choose to. We are able to rationalise experiences and know that we will survive them. We have strategies to solve difficult situations and the benefit of life experiences to know that things usually pass and life does not stay challenging forever. We can choose to talk to people and get support if and when we need it. How difficult are any of these for a 7-year-old to do? Is it therefore surprising that they communicate their feelings and need for support through their behaviour? As adults, the more understanding we can have of what a child may be trying to communicate to us through their behaviour, the greater the chance of the child being understood and being able to make sense of their thoughts and feelings and the more compassion adults can have for them. Children are often very alone with overwhelming thoughts and feelings and this can be a lonely and terrifying experience.

Children communicate a range of different feelings through their behaviour and these can be expressed in many different ways; for example, if a child is scared they may hide under the table or pretend they are not bothered (see Table 3.1).

Table 3.1 Understanding behaviour

Behaviour	Possible feeling
Hiding under table	Scared
Following adult around school	Lonely
Throwing objects	Angry
Hitting someone	Frustrated
Fiddling with something	Anxious
Challenging an adult	Terrified
Criticising another child	Jealous
Saying they don't care	Embarrassed
Chewing their jumper	Worried
Copying another child's work	Sense of failure

Children's internal dialogue

Some children may have learned to respond in a defensive way as a coping mechanism to manage the feelings of anxiety and fear that situations evoke in them. The child may present as feeling the opposite of this, for example, not scared and not bothered, but he may have learned to do this as a way of not feeling pain. 'If I pretend I don't care then I can't be hurt or feel pain.' For this child the silent pain of feeling unwanted or unloved can result in them feeling isolated, confused, frightened and alone. They may feel that everything that happens is their fault and have an internal dialogue that asks 'Am I a bad person? Am I unlovable? Why do I get it wrong all the time? Why can't I do anything right?' When children have this internal belief system and are convinced that they do not deserve anything good, they may go to extreme lengths to prove it.

The combination of their feelings of low self-worth along with a negative internal dialogue not surprisingly may result in challenging and disruptive behaviour as the child tries to bury their feelings and silence their internal voice. They may also actively try to sabotage situations to re-create the feelings and experiences that are familiar to them. Children who have a negative internal dialogue may believe that adults do not like them when they reprimand them. These children may find it difficult to hold on to positive thoughts about themselves as they do not have an internal view of themselves as a good person. School staff can play an essential role in helping to rewrite their internal scripts into a positive dialogue. For example, 'If Mrs Hawkins thinks I'm a kind person maybe I am.' It is crucial that we focus on the positives for these children, no matter how hard this may be to implement and sustain.

Staff strategy – encouraging children to reflect on their behaviour

Provide children with a time out sheet to draw or write about a situation and ask them the following questions:

- What did I do?
- How do I feel?
- What can I do if this happens again?
- Who can I talk to?

Responding to behaviour

Children do not want negative comments or attention for challenging behaviour, but some children may have learned that any attention is better than no attention and therefore may evoke negative reactions from adults. For example, a child that constantly calls out in class may be doing this behaviour to ensure that they stay noticed. It is a guaranteed way of ensuring that they receive attention and are remembered. This may tell us about the child's experiences outside school, why do they need to ensure that they are noticed and remembered at school? Do they have a different experience at home? When children are happy and settled they do not need to ensure that adults notice and remember them; if they do this it is an indication that they need additional help and support.

It can be hard for some children to tolerate their feelings and this can result in them trying to get rid of them rather than accepting and trying to understand and process them. For example, a child who is unable to manage feeling angry may hit another child or throw something as a way of trying to get rid of that feeling. Children need help and support from adults to realise that it is natural to have feelings and that they can be helped to understand how to recognise and express them. It can be useful to integrate positive messages about feelings throughout the school day such as 'All feelings are useful as they tell us something is wrong.' This validates their experiences and normalises how children may be feeling.

This following activity can be integrated into the school day and carried out with the whole class to help them settle after break or lunchtime or when they are anxious or unsettled. It can take about 5 minutes but can be longer or shorter to suit the time available. If children laugh or mess about they may be showing that they feel uncomfortable and it can help to acknowledge this by saying 'This may feel a bit strange at first but let's practise it as I think it will help us feel more relaxed.' If this behaviour continues they are showing you they need more help with this so they could practise it in a smaller group with an adult.

Staff strategy – a grounding activity to help children feel settled

Ask each child to find a space by their table or on the carpet and stand with their feet slightly apart. They can choose whether to have their eyes open or closed. Ask them to focus on their feet, noticing how each toe feels and guide them through this: how does your left foot feel, focus on your little toe, then the toe next to it, etc. Now focus on your left knee, notice how it feels, then your right knee, now your stomach, left arm, right arm, left hand, each finger, left shoulder, right shoulder, neck, left ear, right ear. Ask the children to notice how it feels after you have named each body part.

Use a quiet and gentle voice throughout the activity.

End the activity asking them to do a very gentle stretch with both arms and smile.

For school staff it can be a huge challenge to look beyond the behaviour and attempt to understand what the child may be feeling. It can be easy to judge children for their behaviour as the following comments demonstrate:

- He's just attention-seeking.
- She's being manipulative.
- He never stops talking.
- She's such a good child.
- He's so helpful.
- She's so immature.
- He never speaks.
- She never listens.

However, if adults are able to meet a child's need to be noticed and remembered in a positive and supportive way they may reduce or even stop the behaviour. For example, 'I know it's really hard for you not to call out so I am going to help you with this and give you something to help you to practise.'

Staff strategy – learning to wait

If a child keeps calling out in class offer to help them with this by giving them a sand timer. Ask them to turn it over and watch the sand until it is empty and wait before they speak. Acknowledge and reward them for their efforts and achievements with this.

This activity gives the child something to focus on and can help to reduce their anxiety. It may also meet their need to be noticed as they have a connection to the adult through the timer along with the acknowledgement of their efforts and achievements. After a while the child may learn and start to trust that they are able to get help from an adult with their feelings and to be remembered without having to remind staff.

What are children trying to communicate?

When children show us their feelings through their behaviour it is important that we not only try to understand what they may be feeling and trying to communicate to us, but also that we provide them with an emotional vocabulary to help them to talk about their experiences. For example, when a child says they do not want to do something they may be telling us they are scared.

How often as adults may we decide we don't want to do something when the real reason may be that we are scared? It can be useful to respond by saying, 'I know you are saying that you don't want to do that, but sometimes it can feel a bit frightening to try new things.' Although the child may adamantly deny they are experiencing any fear, it is still helpful to tentatively introduce the idea that this can sometimes contribute to our resistance. If a child uses a baby voice to ask for something or talk to us they may be telling us they are feeling small and vulnerable. When a child fidgets, rocks on their chair, taps things or wriggles on the carpet they are again telling us something. It may be they are telling us they feel worried, anxious or stressed. A response such as 'I can see you are finding it hard to stay still at the moment', can be enough to help a child relax as it communicates that you have noticed them without reprimanding them.

Staff strategy – find the feeling

To help children to identify how they feel, the use of a feelings board at regular intervals during the day can help them. Ask them to draw a face under the word in each box to show the feeling and attach an arrow with a paper fastener in the middle of the square. Ask the child to move the arrow to the relevant feeling.

Happy	Sad

Angry	Scared

This can help children to connect with their feelings more easily and provide permission for the child to experience all their feelings as acceptable.

Helping children to reconnect

Children who live in noisy and chaotic families may tune out and be in their own world as a way of finding some internal peace. At school they may appear not to be listening and may seem disengaged and disinterested. If a child has developed this behaviour as a coping strategy in order to make it easier to live with chaos, we need to be supportive of this and ensure we approach it sensitively. For example, gentle reminders such as a tap on the arm can help them to reconnect with the present moment. The school staff's increased awareness of the possible reasons behind children's behaviour can ensure they offer the appropriate support for the situation. For example, if a child says they feel unwell on a regular basis it may be an indication of stress or anxiety. Children may find it hard to differentiate between physical and emotional pain, they just know they do not feel well. Expressions such as 'sick with fear' are realistic for children who do not have the emotional vocabulary or understanding to separate physical from emotional discomfort (see Table 3.2).

Table 3.2 Links between physical and emotional well-being

Physical feeling	Possible emotional reason
Headache	Worried
Sickness	Fear
Stomach ache	Anxiety

Children may create their own rituals which they demonstrate at school to enable them to feel secure, such as going to the toilet at a particular time of the day or having to sit on the same chair. This behaviour may indicate anxiety and fear and will only be alleviated when the child feels safer. Wherever possible, unless it impacts on another child, it will help the child if this behaviour can be accepted and attention given to helping them feel settled and secure, rather than trying to change their behaviour.

Staff strategy – feeling settled

Offer an object such as a small figure or animal to the child to look after during the day and keep in their drawer overnight. This can help a child to feel more settled and safer at school. Encourage them to give it a name if they wish to, to provide them with a sense of ownership.

The object can also be offered to children who are usually settled and happy at school but are dealing with a change of circumstance at home such as moving house or the arrival of a new baby. The additional comfort offered by the object may help them to adjust to the change more easily and manage their feelings of fear and anxiety.

The cycle of misunderstanding

Case study

Clare, aged 9, always pushed her way to the front of the dinner queue, knocking other children out of the way and hurting them in the process. This resulted in her being reprimanded, asked to apologise and spending lunchtimes on her own, as the other children avoided her. Clare's behaviour resulted in her not getting any of her needs met as she had to go to the back of the line and wait even longer for her lunch. She felt lonely and sad as the other children refused to play with her. Clare was telling herself she was a bad person as the teacher had reprimanded her, and therefore she assumed that the teacher didn't like her.

Possible reasons for Clare's behaviour:

- She never had breakfast at home as things were chaotic.
- She panicked that there wouldn't be enough food for her if she wasn't at the front of the line.
- She was so overwhelmed by hunger that she had no awareness of the other children.
- She wasn't able to say that she was really hungry and was terrified that she may have to go without food.

How often in schools do we see scenarios like this where children are trying to show us what they need or how they feel and they are misunderstood and they get the opposite of what they need? The cycle of misunderstanding demonstrates an all too common scenario in schools (see Figure 3.1).

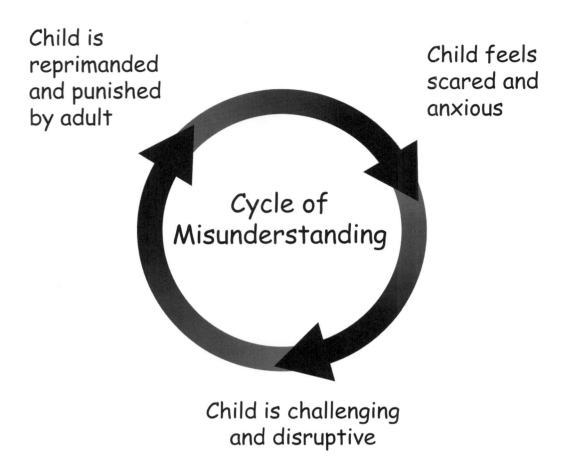

Child is reprimanded and punished by adult

Child feels scared and anxious

Cycle of Misunderstanding

Child is challenging and disruptive

Figure 3.1 The cycle of misunderstanding

However, as has been discussed previously, for some children the contrast between behavioural expectations at home and school is huge. There is a conflict between acceptable behaviour at school and acceptable behaviour at home. The norms of behaviour and morality that are developed at home can be poles apart from what is required at school and many children struggle hugely with this, only to be left with a sense of alienation as they get it wrong once again.

Children learn to develop their own coping strategies to manage their anxiety and this can manifest in different ways from being disruptive and aggressive to being withdrawn and shut down. It can be a challenge for school staff to try and work out what are the possible reasons for the child's behaviour, as well as trying to work out the best way to deal with it. The child's behaviour can often result in an outcome that increases their anxiety rather than reduces it. It can be useful to consider where the child is emotionally rather than developmentally anxious as this can help to understand some of their behaviour, which may be more appropriate for a child of a younger age (see Table 3.3).

Table 3.3 What is this behaviour telling us?

Behaviour	What the child has learned
Class clown	I need to get people to notice me and make them laugh and use humour to get them to like me
Bossy	I need to control things such as people, objects and tasks in order to feel safe
Perfectionist	I need to get things right, it's not ok to make mistakes and I need to do things in a particular way to feel safe
Bully	I need to make other people feel bad in order to make myself feel better because I think I am a bad person
Disengaged	Being in my own head and in my own world is familiar and the safest place to be
Fidgety	Fiddling with things helps me to feel safe and I feel scared and anxious when I can't do this

The above examples provide possible reasons why children have learned particular behaviours as coping strategies to deal with their feelings. If a child needs to have an object to play with or brings in an object from home, it enables school staff to develop a greater understanding of how the child feels. Children who bring in objects from home may be telling us they need help to feel safe at school. If a child was able to put those feelings into words, it would be easier for adults to empathise and support them.

Case study

Kane, aged 10, had frequent tantrums in class if he couldn't get his own way. He would snap pencils and damage other equipment, attacking other children verbally and destroying his own work. After the tantrums he would sit with his head in his hands and sob.

Possible reasons for Kane's behaviour:

- He had witnessed domestic violence between his parents for the first seven years of his life, resulting in him operating at an emotionally younger age.
- He felt scared and unsafe if he wasn't in control.
- He had learned to use controlling and bullying as a way to manage his anxiety.
- He felt so awful about himself that he sabotaged his own work.

Kane's teacher was encouraged to reflect on the possible reasons behind the behaviour while maintaining clear and firm boundaries with him. 'I can see that you are getting really cross, you look furious, but it's not ok to hurt other people. We need to find another way for you to have your feelings and not hurt anyone.' This response provides a clear message to Kane that he is important. The teacher is validating rather than dismissing his feelings and is offering him support with expressing them, thereby breaking the cycle of misunderstanding (see Figure 3.2).

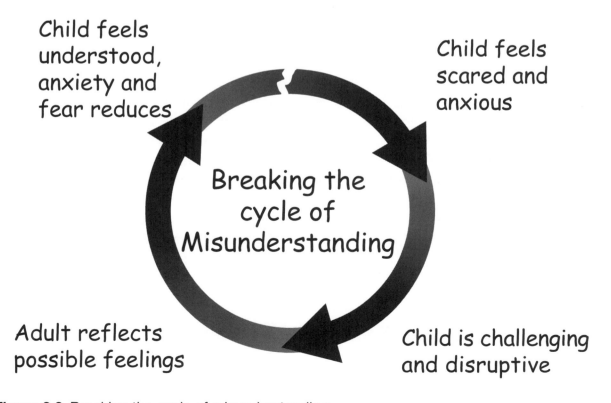

Figure 3.2 Breaking the cycle of misunderstanding

Using reflective language

Throughout this chapter and the rest of the book I provide examples of ways of using reflective language. Reflective language conveys to the child that you are seeing them, trying to understand them and acknowledging any feelings they may be experiencing. It enables adults to tentatively explore the child's experience without making judgements or assumptions about it. Using reflective language clearly communicates to a child 'I see you, I hear you, I am trying to understand you', and enables them to feel seen, heard, valued and understood. For some children this can be a relatively new experience for them and may result in increased self-worth and self-esteem.

Reflect: How could you respond?

Tyreece, aged 10, was often reluctant to get changed for PE, was always last in the line and reluctant to participate in any of the activities.

   Think about how you could use reflective language to gently explore how he is feeling.

Reflective language is a core concept of the group work programme and is key to its success. By using this with children, adults are providing a positive message to them, 'You are worth thinking about and trying to understand, I am trying to help you to work out how you feel and support you with understanding and managing your feelings.' It can be beneficial to use reflective language rather than always reprimanding children or telling them what to do, because it acknowledges and validates the child's feelings and experiences.

Case study

Jamie, aged 9, always wanted to sit in the same seat next to the teaching assistant who was facilitating the self-esteem group. He struggled to sit still and would fidget and tap his finger at the start of each session until he knew what they were doing that week; he was then able to relax and focus on the task.

Possible reasons for Jamie's behaviour:

- His home life was unpredictable with no structure or routine.
- He had moved school three times.
- His class teacher was on long-term sick leave.
- He wasn't able to say that he felt scared and anxious when he didn't know what was going to happen next.

The teaching assistant, rather than reprimand him, was encouraged to reflect on his behaviour: 'I can see that it's really difficult for you to sit still and relax until you know what we are going to do.' This reflection gave a strong and positive message to Jamie that he was worth thinking about and trying to understand.

Children who find it difficult to show their feelings

This can occur when children have learned to internalise rather than externalise their feelings. It can make it more difficult for them to cope at school and to build friendships. They may present as quiet and withdrawn or uncaring and find it hard to show any emotion. Their facial expression may remain the same throughout the day as the events and circumstances around them change; for example, a child who shows no remorse when they have hurt another child and appears to have no understanding of other people's feelings. It can be very difficult for a child to understand other people's feelings if they have little or no understanding of their own.

A child who finds it hard to show feelings may also have learned to bury their physical pain along with their emotional discomfort. They may have learned that no matter how much something hurts it is not safe to make a fuss or ask for help. For example, a child who falls over in the playground and has a large graze on their arm that is bleeding, but continues playing and doesn't appear to notice.

Children who feel unsafe

In order for children to achieve any success at school they need to feel both physically and emotionally safe. While this is essential for any child, if a child experiences their world outside school as unsafe they may be vigilantly looking for evidence that the same is true at school. They may present at school as children who are eager to please and are constantly trying to work out what to do and what to say in order to get it right and please other people. In class they may be noticeable for their attentiveness as they can often be watching everything that is happening. They may be the last person to carry out an instruction because they are watching what everyone else is doing first in order to make sure they get it right and to ensure that the adult meant what they said. For example, the class are asked to go to their drawer, get their reading book, turn to page 27 and start reading. The child who feels unsafe may still be standing at their drawer looking at everyone else while the rest of the class are absorbed in reading. This child needs support with this and is not deliberately being slow or difficult. They are communicating their need to check things out all the time and a gentle reminder of what they need to do can help with their anxiety about this. For example, 'I can see you are standing by your drawer, Joel, and checking to see what everyone is doing; remember to get your book out and go to your seat, then I'll come over and help you find the page.'

This type of behaviour can also be common in children that are so scared and anxious that they are unable to retain much information in their head. This may present itself as a child that is in their own world, not listening and disengaged. They may have their own anxiety-filled internal dialogue in their head which may be punctuated with lots of 'what if' terrifying scenarios. The life experiences for children who demonstrate this behaviour may have been filled with real terrifying scenarios and so their experience of the world is that awful things are always happening. You may get glimpses of a child's anxieties, especially around periods of change. For example, on the day of the school trip they ask what will happen if the coach doesn't turn up or the zoo is closed. This snapshot into their internal world can help us understand how unsafe they feel and to understand their experiences of good things going wrong. They need to be met with patience, support, understanding and reassurance to help contain some of their feelings for them.

Staff strategy – to help a child who can't retain instructions

Use a small whiteboard to list the instructions on and encourage the child to wipe them off when they have accomplished them.

Children who display controlling behaviour

The reasons why a child may display controlling behaviour are many and varied. A child who bullies other children may be being bullied, dominated and controlled at home. They may be witnessing behaviour outside school that demonstrates to them how to control and manipulate other people. For example, a child who has controlling parents who do not allow the child to make any decisions or to have any choice or control over anything in their life, may also demonstrate this behaviour at school. A child who bullies other children needs help to find other ways to feel powerful and good about themselves. It is useful to explore how the child may feel about themselves as children with confidence and self-esteem who feel good about themselves do not need or want to bully other children.

Staff strategy – book of achievements

Divide the class list into five days of the week and tell the children you are going to ask them to share something they have achieved or tried to do on their allocated day. At the end of the day before the class leaves, ask the chosen 5 or 6 children to tell the rest of the class and ask the class to applaud. Ask them to write it in their book of achievements and each child will have approximately 38 by the end of the year.

Children who demonstrate controlling behaviour towards other children, such as trying to turn other children against them or manipulating them into doing what they want them to, need the opportunity to experience success in other more positive ways. Children bring their own experiences of success and failure, fairness and justice with them to school, and, depending on how these match the school experience, they may impact on their behaviour. When a child experiences conflict between these two experiences from home and school it can make it very hard for them to manage the differences, which is explored in more detail in Chapter Two. If a child is constantly challenging school staff it is an indication that they need help to build and sustain relationships. This is discussed in more detail in Chapter Five.

Children who have difficulty communicating

When a child finds it hard to communicate they need additional support to articulate their needs. If a child has English as a second language or is a selective mute, it is essential they are provided with the tools to help them to express their thoughts, needs and feelings. From the child's perspective, school life may be very frightening and confusing and these feelings may manifest in their behaviour. If a child chooses not to speak at school it is important to work on helping to reduce their anxiety rather than focusing on how to get them to talk.

Staff strategy – helping a child who chooses not to speak at school

- Offer them a notepad to write or draw in if they want to communicate with you; this can feel less intimidating than face-to-face conversations.
- Explore using picture cards to help them communicate their needs, e.g. Water bottle, toilet, etc.
- Encourage them to choose a job to do in class with another child to help build relationships with other children.

Children who need help managing their feelings

When children are having tantrums and are raging, their bodies are having a physical response that can exacerbate the situation if it is not responded to appropriately by an adult. Some children fight with others or throw things when they are anxious or scared, others will try and hide or run off. The reactions can either be fight, wanting to fight against the feelings and bodily sensations, or flight, wanting to run away from them. Children who run out of class and/or hide around school are clearly communicating that they need help with their feelings. They may be saying 'I feel overwhelmed, terrified and unsafe and I need help to stop feeling like this.' If we respond to this behaviour by bringing the child back to class without helping them with their feelings we are almost guaranteed that things will deteriorate as the day goes on. A response such as 'It's a shame you did that, how can I help you to make a different choice?' may diffuse the situation more easily.

Case study

Jacob, aged 8, was leaving his class several times a day. He was so adept at doing it that his teacher sometimes didn't notice as he would sneak out when she was using the whiteboard or crawl along the floor if she was working with a group. At other times he would just run. He had a variety of hiding places in his large school which was an old building with plenty of space. The school staff would often spend a long time looking for him.

Possible reasons for his behaviour:

- He had moved house and school four times and found school work difficult.
- He felt overwhelmed and scared he would be in trouble if he couldn't do something so he wanted to escape from his feelings of anxiety and fear.
- He had witnessed domestic violence at home and was used to making a den under his bed for him and his younger brother to hide in when they felt unsafe.

If a child is finding it difficult to stay in class it can help to create a den or calm space for them to go to in the class. This enables them to gradually regulate their feelings and access their learning again when they feel calmer and safer. There may be concerns from school staff that all the children in the class will want to go in the den, or that the child will want to sit in there all day and use it as an excuse not to do their work. However, in my experience this is not the case and rules for the use of the space can be agreed with the child. The situation can be used as an opportunity to explore the differences that exist in the class and to discuss situations that children may need help with. For example, 'Some children go out every day with Miss Giles to have extra help with their numeracy and other children need help with different things. The calm space is to help Jacob to have some time out when he needs it and we can all help him with this. Jacob is an important person in our class and we want to make it easier for him to stay in our class all day. Remember in this class we are really good at helping each other with things.'

When a child has had help managing their feelings and some time out to calm down they may feel safer and be able to access their learning again, rather than their anxiety and fear increasing and their behaviour deteriorating. It is a huge challenge to expect a child who has left the class to just walk in and return to their learning without any help or support from an adult. If an adult walked out of work or left a training course because they were upset, it would be extremely hard for them to just walk back in and carry on as though nothing had happened.

Staff strategy – creating a calm space in the classroom

Ideally this will be a small area against a wall in a corner of the room, with cushions on the floor and a bookcase or table to create a sense of it being separate from the class and enclosed. It can have a sand timer, soft toys and a snowstorm or other soothing objects.

Explain to the child that you are going to make an area in class for them to help them when things feel difficult or scary. Ask if they would like to help you make it and talk to them about how they can use it. For example, 'I know that sometimes it can feel very hard for you when we are doing our writing and it may make you feel anxious and scared. This is a place you can come to when you have those feelings and then Mr Clark or I will come and see if we can help you. This may help to make it easier for you to stay in the class with us and we'd all like it if that happened.'

You can set rules around the amount of time and how it can be used with the individual child according to their needs.

Children who have difficulty regulating stress may find it hard to tolerate excitement, resulting in them sabotaging events such as a school trip or Christmas party. In order to help children with this it is necessary to understand the feelings behind the behaviour. A child who associates Christmas or parties as a time that starts off happy but often ends in disaster may find it impossible to believe the experience will be any different at school. If a child is clearly showing that they are trying to destroy an event it is useful to ask them to do a job or offer the opportunity to help in a nursery or reception class with younger children while the preparations are taking place. This can help to manage their anxieties and ensure they do not create a situation that results in them missing the event due to their behaviour. These children need to experience positive examples of events that they associate with negative outcomes to provide them with alternative evidence and experiences.

During the group work training I deliver I encourage staff to think about the reason and the feeling behind the behaviour. When an adult is able to stop and think about the reason for the child's behaviour and what they may be feeling, instead of reacting instantly and making assumptions, they are beginning to put the child and their emotional needs first. By tentatively reflecting and commenting on what they are observing, the adult is providing a powerful message to the child about the validity of their feelings and opening up opportunities for exploring alternative ways of dealing with them. The group work programme in this book provides a structured way for school staff to be able to integrate this into their way of working with children.

4 Integrating emotional well-being into the whole school

In the previous chapters I discussed the importance of consistency in helping a child to develop emotionally and feel safe and secure at school. In order to be most effective, this consistent approach involves the whole school, is integrated into the curriculum and includes all staff from lunchtime organisers to head teachers. A whole school approach to emotional health and well-being is a key component of achieving success for individual children within the school. When considering the emotional health and well-being approach that a school is going to use, it is essential for the head teacher to ensure it can be filtered easily across the school and embedded into the ethos.

Whole school approach

In order to identify the success of a school it is useful to explore whether the children are happy, settled and achieving their full potential, along with identifying any barriers to being able to achieve this. Throughout their day at school children are expected to deal with a variety of challenges such as trying new things, separating from their parents, etc. The way the school responds to the children's reactions to these events can influence their outcome. The school day is full of experiences that may evoke feelings in children and expose them to new and difficult situations. We may expect children to manage these without showing any response or reaction and, thus, may be surprised when they do. Children's fears need to be listened to and validated so they feel safe enough to voice them. School staff can develop self-awareness to ensure they are not being dismissive by using phrases such as 'don't be silly'. This can be discounting of the child's feelings and can exacerbate the child's fears (see Table 4.1).

Table 4.1 Potential emotional impact of the school day

Situation	Feeling
Leave their parent	Scared
Follow rules	Overwhelmed
Listen to instructions	Confused
Manage changes such as having a new teacher	Terrifying
Eat lunch in a large hall	Intimidating

The messages that children receive from the school environment and school staff can also reinforce how they view themselves and how they experience the world. These experiences can provide subtle messages about issues such as trust and responsibility by small everyday tasks. For example, if a child is asked to deliver a note to another teacher they are given the message 'I can trust you' and 'You can be responsible'.

Making assumptions

Schools have a commitment to assessing each child's literacy and numeracy levels and providing additional support through interventions such as booster groups for children who may need it. However, in terms of social and emotional development they do not assess a child's social skills but may sometimes reprimand them if they have difficulty in this area. We may expect children to be at a certain developmental level and make assessments based on their chronological rather than social and emotional age. For example, a 7-year-old who finds it difficult to share with others may be operating at an emotional level of a 3-year-old. It can be useful to consider the social and emotional skills that we may assume children have as we may think they are able to share, listen, cooperate, sit quietly, sit still, work with others and follow instructions. We can make assumptions that a child's age and developmental level are linked and for some children there can be a big gap in this being a reality. Does your school provide extra help and support in other areas, yet punish or reprimand children for not having the skills we expect them to have in others?

School staff may also presume that a child has a level of language and a cognitive understanding of the meaning of certain words. For some children skills such as empathy and consideration are difficult to understand and even harder to put into practice. When children are operating at a much younger age in terms of their social and emotional development they require extra support and clear explanations to enable them to achieve this. The group work programmes in this book can be used to enable children who need extra support to develop age-appropriate behaviour.

Opportunities in the school day

Throughout the course of a school day there are many situations that may enable children to feel good about themselves and to achieve success. These opportunities may need to be adapted to enable every child to experience positive results, just as we are able to differentiate a child's learning to achieve this. An example of this can be a 'Star of the day award' that can be presented to a child in class at the end of each day. This is an excellent way to ensure that every child receives this award at some point as it can be given for effort made, being kind, etc. rather than achieving a specific goal. There are also opportunities at school for children to experience disappointment and failure and for school staff to help them with the feelings these situations may evoke. This is an important aspect of developing resilience. The task of all adults in school is to acknowledge these feelings as they occur and help the child to manage them. It is important not to let a child win a game every time they play with an adult as this is unrealistic and will not build resilience. It is far better to help the child understand that everyone wins and loses at times and to help them explore and express their feelings about this. This can help them to develop persistence, determination and motivation rather than feeling overwhelmed and devastated. As discussed in previous chapters, this can be easier for some children to achieve due to their life experiences, and an individual needs-led approach can support this process.

Lunchtime

Lunchtimes in schools can be the most challenging part of the day, especially if the weather results in children having to be kept inside. The lunch period can be a difficult time for children as it is generally less structured and may feel disorganised and chaotic. This can be especially hard for children whose home lives may mirror this. The most effective way of managing this situation is to link a lunchtime organiser with each class who will ideally follow that class through the school, so there is some consistency of staff for the children. This can be difficult to implement as the lunchtime staff team may change frequently as staff leave the school. However, the more the staff feel they are an essential part of the school, and have the opportunity to have their thoughts and feelings listened to, the more likely they are to continue working at the school. It is essential that all staff feel valued and appreciated in their role, including the lunchtime staff.

They also need opportunities to develop skills and expertise and to be provided with guidance and support. A large amount of the afternoon session in school can be spent sorting out incidents that have happened over the lunchtime. This can be drastically reduced by equipping the lunchtime staff with support and the tools to understand and manage behaviour. Staff can focus on telling children what they do not want them to do, rather than making it clear what they should be doing. Instead, try replacing don't with do and see whether this makes a difference.

Staff strategy for lunchtime organisers

As a staff team, work in pairs and compile a list of examples of behaviour that you may ask children not to do; e.g. Don't push when you are in the dinner queue. Change each example into the behaviour you would like to see:

Don't	Do
Don't push when you are in the dinner queue.	Thank you for lining up nicely.

Compile a list of the behaviour you would like to see and ensure you all use it each day to provide consistency across the school. Meet with the team again and review whether you have noticed a difference in the children's behaviour.

Managing changes in the school day

As mentioned in previous chapters, the experience of consistency and predictability is essential for children's emotional well-being. Class teachers can contribute to this by acknowledging any changes throughout the day, for example, ensuring their class know when they are having their preparation time during the week. This can be helped further if the teacher returns to class afterwards to say goodbye to the children at the end of the day. This may result in the class being able to manage their teacher's absence more easily, and improved behaviour, knowing they will be returning at the end of the day to check on the class and review the afternoon. It is also possible for schools to use a similar approach when they are employing a supply teacher for the day. For example, the class teacher could leave a note to be read to the class at the start of the day. This would enable the class to manage their feelings more easily and provide a sense of predictability for them.

Dear Class Five,

Remember that I am on a course today to learn more exciting ways that I can teach you science. I will be back in class tomorrow morning and look forward to seeing you all then. I hope you all have a good day and show your supply teacher what a great class you are.

Mrs Omoboye

In order to ensure there is a consistent approach to behaviour and class expectations any supply staff that are covering staff absences can also be provided with guidelines to manage behaviour. A supply teacher who manages behaviour by intimidating children or shouting can undo the ethos the school is trying to create. For example, 'In this school we encourage positive behaviour by acknowledging and praising the behaviour we would like to see increasing and find it helps the children if all staff use a calm, clear voice rather than shouting.'

Transition

As discussed in previous chapters, some children find any change extremely difficult as it can evoke feelings of loss, anxiety and uncertainty. It is useful therefore that children's transitions to new classes are managed with patience and understanding. For a child who has experienced many changes and uncertainty in their life outside school, the transition to a new class and new teacher can be overwhelming. Children have to adapt to a new relationship, maybe a different way of working and a new classroom environment, all at the end of spending six weeks away from school.

The first two weeks of term can be very challenging for children and staff and an important time to focus on developing and building the new relationship. This enables them to feel safe and to relax and engage with their learning. If this is not prioritised it can be very difficult to retrace and rebuild this. It is important that this is a gradual process and that allowances are made for children who may have difficulty building a new relationship.

Staff strategy – making a connection

Provide an opportunity for each child to make a 'getting to know me' poster to be given to their new teacher before their new class transition day. Encourage them to write or draw things they are happy for their new teacher to know about them. For example, I love bananas and my favourite colour is red. Their new teacher can spend time with each child on that day and share their poster with them. This can be a good way of making an initial connection with each child in a relaxed way. As the focus is on the poster, it can help children who find new relationships frightening and overwhelming.

The role of school staff

A beneficial tool for all school staff is the ability to reflect on themselves and their practice in an honest and open manner and consider how it may feel to be a child in their school. In order for them to do this they need to feel safe and reassured that their observations will be heard and responded to in a supportive way. This can start with the head teacher and other senior members of staff and filter down the school to the lunchtime organisers and office staff. The relationships and professionalism between staff across the school can create either a supportive and effective team or a divided group of people who are all struggling to go to work every day.

Qualities to develop in all staff

- Are all staff approachable?
- Are they supportive to each other?
- Can they rely on each other?
- Do they work as a team or compete against each other?
- Are they open and receptive to change?

- Are they honest about themselves and their work?
- Do they maintain professionalism and confidentiality?
- Are they able to reflect and admit their mistakes?
- Are they motivated and committed to the children and the school?
- Do they model good working practice?
- Are they resilient?

Staff training

The experience of high quality inspirational training is of paramount importance for all staff in school and opportunities to access additional training relevant to their role need to be available to all staff. The impact of this experience can be filtered across the school and new ideas and initiatives may be met with excitement and enthusiasm. Staff can be supported with identifying relevant training by formal and informal discussions and feedback on their performance. I feel it is beneficial to give feedback to staff on their relationships with children, not just their performance during lesson observations as this is such a crucial aspect of their role in school. The relationships between children and staff are discussed in more detail in Chapter Five.

Staff relationships

The quality of the relationships between staff in school impacts on their ability to work together effectively and to model positive relationships to the children. The relationship between the class teacher, teaching assistant and support workers in their class need to be harmonious to ensure they are able to work together effectively. The relationship between staff working in the same class needs to incorporate open and honest communication along with mutual respect and appreciation. This can be demonstrated in front of the children so they are able to experience the impact of relating to other people in this way. When children have experienced living with disharmony and conflict they are more receptive to noticing this in other relationships.

If the relationship between staff is one of mistrust, resentment and animosity then this may be witnessed by the children through verbal and non-verbal interactions. When a child feels there is conflict between staff they may become preoccupied with trying to resolve this, rather than engaging with their learning. This may occur if a child is familiar with playing the role of peace maker and negotiator at home. Some children are very tuned in to relationships and will recognise atmospheres and behaviours between staff that can make them worried and anxious. Children need school to be a haven where they feel safe and protected and any negative feelings between staff and a difficult atmosphere will prevent this from happening. There are opportunities to show children how to manage feelings and conflict between people through the relationships between all staff across the school.

Staff morale

Adults working in school need to feel valued and supported in their work in order to be productive, and the morale of the staff can impact on the children in a positive or negative way. All adults working in school have a responsibility to create a happy and relaxed atmosphere for children, or to decide what they can do to change it. Working in schools can be a demanding and exhausting but rewarding and enjoyable job. In order for staff to work most effectively and give their best to the children they need to feel happy and fulfilled. It is important they feel they are making a difference and that they are an essential cog in the wheel of school life. The school needs to be emotionally safe for staff in order to be emotionally safe for children.

Appropriate staff behaviour

As mentioned previously, the messages we are communicating to children as adults have a significant impact on them. When working in schools it is necessary for staff to have awareness of how their behaviour may influence the children on a daily basis. Staff whose behaviour is loud and outgoing may unnerve and intimidate children who may easily experience adults as frightening and overwhelming. If staff constantly joke and laugh with children it is important to check that they understand when you are being serious. It is our job as adults to decide and implement the boundaries around this for children and not to reprimand them if they become over excited. Some children are overly aware of what adults are saying and doing and may look for hidden clues in people's behaviour. For example, 'Mr Graves looked cross this morning, I think it's because I didn't finish all my maths yesterday.' In reality, the teacher had just heard that the printer was broken.

Reflect: How do I behave?

- Are my interactions always appropriate?
- What is my tone of voice and facial expression communicating?
- Do I have consistent boundaries no matter how I am feeling?

All children react differently to shouting, and while this may get their attention immediately in some situations, it can also provide mixed messages to children. If we reprimand children for shouting or ask them to speak nicely to each other and then children hear staff shouting, we are causing confusion. We are saying one behaviour is acceptable for adults but not for children. There are occasions when it may be necessary for an adult to raise their voice in school; for example, if a child is about to fall or hurt themselves. However, adults may use shouting as a way of trying to manage children's behaviour. For a child who has experienced domestic violence or lives in a family where shouting is used as a way of communicating, this can be a very frightening experience. The child may tune out and appear to not be listening but actually may be feeling scared and unsure what to do. This can create even more anxiety and stress for the child.

Managing feelings

The school setting provides an ideal situation to demonstrate how to express and manage feelings on a daily basis. Staff can model ways of expressing their own feelings, often without being aware of it. Staff who sulk, moan, patronise, and humiliate other members of staff, parents and children are providing powerful messages about how to manage feelings. If schools have clear expectations about children's behaviour and what is acceptable and unacceptable, they need to ensure this is implemented at all times by all staff. For example, a child told me they had heard a teaching assistant swear when they had been asked to cover another class. The child asked me if they would get a verbal warning, i.e. the same consequence that would apply to a child in school. It is essential that schools provide a consistent message to everyone in school and are not contradictory in their approach.

The way that the school staff react to everyday situations provides an opportunity to model ways of dealing with feelings to children. For example, if a member of staff makes a mistake or breaks something, this can be used as an opportunity to acknowledge this happens to everyone and that it is an important part of life. It can offer the chance to explain that mistakes allow us to learn and try things, rather than covering it up so children may think that adults never make mistakes. Throughout the school day there are so many learning opportunities that are not part of the curriculum that can be used for children to learn invaluable life lessons. For example, do adults apologise to children, do they demonstrate the behaviour we want children to have? Do children feel that there is room for them to make mistakes and that they get praise for being brave and trying things?

As adults we all have a responsibility to help children to understand and express their feelings rather than feel scared or overwhelmed by them. There are endless opportunities for school staff to share their experiences of managing their own feelings throughout the day. If there is a commitment from all school staff to use emotional vocabulary and share experiences appropriately with children, this can result in children being able to mirror this behaviour. This can be achieved by acknowledging situations as they arise throughout the day; for example, 'When I try something new I can get a sick feeling in my stomach, I know this is fear and it can help me to talk to someone when I feel like this.' Making statements such as 'Everyone has difficult feelings sometimes and it can help to tell people when we feel like this', can contribute to children's awareness of themselves and other people.

Using reflective language

We can also provide positive messages to children in a subtle way throughout the school day by thinking about and commenting on what is happening by using reflective language to tentatively explore what a child may be experiencing. This is discussed in more detail in Chapter Three.

Table 4.2 Impact of positive reflective responses

Reflective response	Message to child
I've been thinking about how hard it is for you to remember your PE kit	You are worth thinking about
I'm going to ask Mrs Jones to spend some time with you and teach you how to tie your shoelaces; I can see it frustrates you when you try to do them	You are worth helping
It's important that everyone has a turn at being at the front of the line	Your needs matter
You looked sad when you didn't get chosen for the football team; I wonder if you'd like to choose a friend and help me unpack the new books	You are important

The examples of reflective language provided in Table 4.2 enable it to be integrated into the school day. For example, if a child is struggling or finding a task difficult, it can help to reflect 'It can be difficult when we get things wrong' or 'It can feel frustrating when we are trying to do something and we can't work out how to do it.' This enables the child to feel noticed and understood, along with helping them to identify how frustration feels. Over time this enables the child to link the feelings with the word and to make that connection themselves. This may result in them being able to use the word themselves when they next have that feeling. It assists enormously if school staff are able to use this as a way of commenting on their own feelings; for example, 'I felt sad when I was unwell and missed the school trip.' See Chapters Eleven and Twelve for more examples of using reflective language.

Using affirmative language

The use of language is an important aspect of the behaviour approach within school and using affirmative language which focuses on the behaviour you want to see rather than the behaviour you don't is a beneficial approach. For example, 'Please walk down the corridor' rather than 'Don't run' will often be more effective. When we focus on the aspects of behaviour we don't want, then that is what we will see. Children just hear the word 'run' and it gives them an idea, in the same way as we may say to a toddler 'Don't touch the plug', they just hear the word plug and immediately head towards it.

This approach is useful for children who have poor self-regulation and impulse control and may find it extremely difficult to change their behaviour and not do things. For example, if at home a child has to interrupt other people and talk over them to be heard, then it can be difficult not to act in the same way at school. A class teacher recently used the phrase 'Who's being rude' as a way of managing a classroom situation. The child who was talking went red and looked ashamed. A different response such as 'Remember we all need to listen to each other' would not have targeted and shamed the child and may have achieved the same result in a less direct way.

Listening to children

It is useful to consider how much time is allocated to listening to children's thoughts, feelings and ideas during the school day and exploring whether children feel safe enough to do this. It is beneficial to provide opportunities for children to do this throughout the school year and for their ideas to be acknowledged and responded to in a positive and accepting manner. Some children who frequently say 'I don't mind' may have learned this as a way of dealing with being let down and disappointed. They may pretend they don't mind as they have learned 'There is no point saying what I want because I won't get it. It's easier to pretend I don't mind then I don't have to feel disappointed or upset.' These children need regular opportunities to make choices, along with validation that their ideas and feelings matter and are important.

Integrating emotional vocabulary in the curriculum

During the school day children may be asked to experience situations that adults may not feel comfortable experiencing, such as being vulnerable and sharing things about themselves that adults may find difficult to do. For example, asking a child to identify things they struggle with or find difficult. In class an adult may randomly choose a child to answer a question, thereby exposing them in a way we would be uncomfortable with as adults. How many of us have attended training where we would feel uncomfortable if the facilitator randomly singled us out to participate?

Reflect: Would this feel comfortable?

- What do we ask children to do?
- How may it feel for them?
- How would I feel if someone asked me to do this?
- How can we change this to make it feel easier and less intimidating for children?

There are many opportunities during the school day to introduce and familiarise children with emotional vocabulary. It is essential to use this as often as possible so it becomes a recognised way of interacting and avoids children being asked to do something without naming and explaining it. For example, if a child hits another child and is asked why they behaved in this way, it is not realistic to expect them to explain if they are not provided with the appropriate vocabulary to be able to do this. The school staff, ensuring they use regular opportunities to introduce emotional vocabulary to children, can assist them with this.

Choices and responsibility

In school, children are provided with opportunities to learn about making choices and taking responsibility. This has a positive impact on their confidence, self-esteem and self-worth. If children are given choices over small things throughout the day such as choosing to write with a pen or pencil, they are able to understand that with every choice comes a consequence. For example, a child who chooses to write in pencil is able to erase a mistake, whereas a child who choses to write in pen is unable to do this. This can help them to understand more easily about the consequences of other choices they may make, such as choosing to hit someone has a consequence of missing out on playtime.

When we give a child a choice or responsibility we are saying:

● I trust you.
● Your views are important.
● Your needs matter.

Creating the right environment

The physical environment that is created in a school impacts on the emotional well-being of everyone who comes into school. For children who experience disorganisation and unpredictability outside school, the organised and ordered environment of school contributes to their sense of safety and well-being. Classrooms that are clean, tidy and enable children to find things easily and have things in the same place so children can access them easily, provide a sense of stability in children's otherwise unstable lives. A child who returns to school after a chaotic and unstructured weekend can feel soothed by knowing the felt pens will be in the same place on Monday morning. The children can be encouraged to have responsibility for taking care of their class and this can involve a teamwork approach. A sense of ownership and pride can be encouraged across the school but specifically in relation to individual classes. It is important to involve children in this as it is their space and the more comfortable they feel the easier they will find it to engage with their learning.

Within each class the children can have responsibility for their classroom which can be implemented by allocating children to certain areas of the class and compiling a tasks list; for example, tidying the book corner, etc. The children can be given choice over the area, which provides an opportunity to ask them for their ideas about their classroom environment. This can be used to talk about managing differences of opinion and compromise and how to use skills of negotiation. It gives children the message 'we care about our class and each other'. At the end of each half term it can be useful to have a class discussion to review what is working well and why. This gives the children a voice and sense of ownership over their class, along with developing teamwork skills.

Feeling safe and secure at school

School staff may make assumptions and have their own ideas about children's understanding of safety, but it is important to clarify this with them. The staff can also lead by example through their own behaviour and by ensuring that clear explanations are offered to children. For example, if a child is running while holding a pair of scissors they need an example of the alternative behaviour you would like to see along with an explanation of why they need to change their behaviour, such as 'Please walk when you are carrying scissors because if you trip or fall you could hurt yourself and I don't want that to happen.' It is important to be aware of not making assumptions about children's understanding or awareness of safety because of their age. Some children have no sense of danger because they may never have been made aware of it. These children may look confused when explanations about safety are offered to them. Acknowledging that you don't want a child to hurt themselves or that you want to keep them safe, may come as a surprise for some children who may be physically or emotionally hurt by adults outside school.

Staff strategy – increasing awareness of safety

Take children for a safety walk around school and ask them to identify the dangers both inside and in the playground. This enables you to assess each child's awareness and understanding of safety. It may bring you some surprises.

Emotional safety

Schools can play an important role in promoting children's awareness of emotional safety by exploring how we behave towards other people and why. It is beneficial to discuss why we are kind and care for each other and identify the feelings this may evoke. Children need to trust that the adults in school will protect them from harm in order to feel emotionally safe at school. This can be achieved by a clear and consistent policy for dealing with bullying and ensuring it is implemented by all staff. School days can be the best or worst days of our lives and some of this is affected by friendships and peer relationships. It is essential that all children across school understand that any form of bullying is unacceptable and that staff understand that children who bully need urgent help. This is discussed in more detail in Chapter Three and Chapter Five.

An environment where children feel safe enough to make mistakes and are supported to learn from them provides an excellent learning opportunity. However, if a child who accidentally breaks something is reprimanded and punished, they may not only be too scared to admit when they do this in the future, but they may also learn 'It is not ok to make mistakes.' This may prevent them from trying in the future and evoke a sense of shame about their behaviour. If an adult responds with compassion rather than irritation a child learns that making mistakes and breaking things is a part of life.

Behaviour system

The school behaviour system provides the foundations of the school and is most effective when it is implemented consistently across the school in terms of expectations and responses to behaviour. Any inconsistencies between adults may make children feel scared and anxious, resulting in them being quiet and withdrawn or challenging and controlling. This requires a commitment of all staff and an understanding of the importance of this. The behaviour system needs to be clear and understandable by children across the school and the behavioural expectations for the school to be realistic and achievable by all the children to enable everyone to achieve success. It is useful to ask the children for feedback on their understanding of it and how it works to ensure it has been understood. For example, if a child is regularly having difficulty following a particular rule, encourage the class teacher or another adult in school to check their understanding of it.

Helping children to understand behavioural expectations

It is important not to make assumptions about a child's understanding of behaviour without assessing it, just as we would assess their literacy or numeracy. For example, if a school rule is 'We are kind and gentle with each other', it is important to give the children examples of how they can achieve this. Some of the expectations we have about children's behaviour in school may make it very difficult for them to achieve success. For example, during assembly children may be expected to sit on a sometimes cold, hard floor and are reprimanded for being unable to do this without fidgeting or moving about. Most adults would find this difficult, yet we expect children to manage it. There may be limited alternatives as there may not be enough chairs for children, but if staff can acknowledge that it's a difficult thing to do, they are at least validating the children's experience.

To create an effective school environment the attributes shown in Table 4.3 are useful.

Table 4.3 Useful attributes

Staff need	Children need
Patience	Understanding
Encouragement	Nurturing
Motivation	Consistency
Determination	Support
Support	Praise
Commitment	Encouragement
Tolerance	Recognition

It is essential in schools that school staff attempt to explore why children are behaving in particular ways, what they may be trying to communicate, how they feel and what can be done to help them with this. The more that children can feel understood and supported in trying to change their behaviour, the increased likelihood there is that this will happen. Imagine as adults if no one ever tried to understand us or help us to make changes, how would that feel?

Using behaviour charts

Behaviour charts are an invaluable way of monitoring children's behaviour and providing them with targets to achieve. However, they are most effective when they enable children to achieve some degree of success and to see the immediate results of their efforts. It is unrealistic to give a child more than one target. In the same way as we would not expect an adult to stop smoking, take up running, go on a diet and stop drinking all at the same time, because it would be unrealistic to expect them to achieve and maintain it; we need to apply the same philosophy when setting targets for children. For example, an initial target of 'good listening' for a child can be extended to develop additional changes once the child has experienced success.

Involving parents

Parents play a vital role in the school and for a child to reach their full potential it is essential that they are as involved as possible, have positive experiences of the school and feel valued and supported in their role. It is most effective for the child if the relationship between parents and school is a harmonious one. It is worthwhile to make parents aware of and explain any interventions that are being offered in school so they are able to use a similar approach with their child at home. For example, a parent whose child was involved in the group work friendship programme was able to support this work by encouraging the child to practise the skills at home alongside the group, therefore maximising the potential for change occurring. As the parents in the school became more aware of the group work programmes and their effectiveness, this resulted in increased numbers asking for their children to participate. See Part Two for more information on the group work programme.

Developing life skills

The school setting is the ideal place for children to learn about and practise developing essential life skills and the opportunity to do this can be integrated into the school curriculum through lessons and activities. The possibilities to do this are enormous and enable staff to be creative in their approach along with providing a template for developing and managing relationships. Qualities such as honesty, tolerance, compassion, courage, patience, etc. can all be integrated into the curriculum and develop resilience and other skills. It is important not to make assumptions about the skills that a child may have as this will depend on their external experiences as discussed in more detail in Chapter Two. Children can be helped with skills such as organisation by involving them in working with other children and planning an event such as an end of term party. This is also useful for children who find it hard to work with other people and may find it difficult not being the centre of attention. Working with an adult such as a teaching assistant or learning mentor around a task like this can enable children to develop these skills or expand on existing ones.

The group work programmes in this book provide an important part of an effective whole school approach by creating opportunities for children to have additional support with emotional and social skills along with validating and appreciating their individuality.

For the group work programmes to be most effective, they need to be part of a whole school approach that reinforces the skills and experiences for children and staff. For example, Monique, aged 11, found it difficult to keep friends and could be bossy and controlling towards other children. While she was in the friendship group, the group facilitator met with her mum and Monique each week at the end of the school day to explain the task for that week and to encourage her to support Monique with this. The facilitator also liaised with Monique's class teacher and the teaching assistant in her class, sharing the skills they had been practising in the session. This approach enabled them to encourage her to transfer these skills outside the sessions and provide the additional support she needed. This resulted in her friendships and confidence and self-esteem improving as she felt better about herself. If the group facilitator can liaise regularly with the parents, head teacher, class teacher and other adults working with the children across the school to provide feedback on the child's behaviour and share information, then this enables it to be fully integrated across the school rather than seen as a tokenistic gesture that may be hard to sustain.

5 Developing positive and meaningful relationships at school

Early relational experiences

In order for children to be able to build relationships with other people it is necessary for them to have a template of how to do this. A child's first relationship is with their main caregiver and this is usually a mother, father, grandparent or other relative. The quality of this primary relationship can determine the standard of future relationships. Children who have experienced their first relationship with a parent or carer that is nurturing, supportive, consistent and loving are able to develop an internal feeling of safety and security. This experience enables the child to explore freely and have a natural curiosity and excitement about life. As their early needs for food and stimulation have been responded to and their early interactions through babbling and gurgling have been met with enthusiasm and delight, they learn that their needs are recognised and met and they are worth thinking about and caring for, resulting in high self-esteem. They may present in school as having the skills and ability to build and maintain relationships and respond positively to help and support with this when needed.

However, a child who has had an erratic, inconsistent and unpredictable experience of early relationships may find it more difficult to internalise a sense of safety and security and may experience relationships as frightening and unreliable. If a parent or carer is emotionally or physically unavailable to the child, perhaps rejecting their needs and ignoring them or pushing them away when they cry, the child learns that their needs are not worthwhile and that if you seek comfort from someone you may be rejected. They may present in school as being quiet, withdrawn and self-contained. 'He seems happy on his own', may be how this child is referred to. For these children, relationships are frightening and to be avoided wherever possible, even if it means missing out on positive experiences.

Being a parent can be extremely stressful and challenging at times, and some parents may have little or no experience of receiving positive parenting themselves. A parent or caregiver who is overwhelmed by their own needs or difficulties may find it hard to respond to their child's needs in a consistent and caring way. They may be trying to keep themselves physically and emotionally safe, for example, if they are experiencing domestic violence, and may be unable to meet the needs of their child. Children who have this early experience may respond by being clingy, watchful and mistrusting of people. They may present in school as being controlling and manipulative in order to manage their high levels of anxiety. They may focus on objects rather than people as they are easier to predict and manage; for example, a child who always fiddles with bits of paper or seems to have an endless supply of items in their pocket. This child may need to have these in order to feel safe and secure. It is important for staff working in schools to consider this when removing objects that may appear to be rubbish or to have no significance as they may be of crucial importance and represent security for the child.

Case study

Jordan, aged 9, found it difficult to develop and keep friendships with other children at school. He was controlling and manipulative towards them and wanted to have his own way all the time. He found it impossible to understand any one else's point of view and would become aggressive to other children if they could do something better than him. He avoided any relationships with school staff who experienced him as rude and challenging. He was always playing with blu tack and became agitated and angry when staff attempted to take it from him.

His mum had been involved in a volatile relationship while pregnant with him and for the first three years of his life until she finally separated from his dad. She had also experienced post natal depression and had found it difficult to build a relationship with him, although she loved him and bought him anything he wanted. She was unpredictable in her parenting style which ranged from cold and indifferent to loving and over compensating.

Jordan spent hours in front of the television from being a baby as this appeared to be the only thing that would soothe him. As he got older he developed an interest in computer games, some of which were violent. His mum shared her concerns about his behaviour and said it was getting harder as he got older and resembled his dad more, with whom she still had a challenging relationship and now disliked intensely.

Jordan needs:

- the chance to experience a consistent relationship from a caring adult in school;
- the opportunity to be helped to build friendships with other children;
- to build his confidence and self-esteem in order to experience a more positive sense of himself;
- for school staff to understand why he needs his blu tack and for him to be allowed to keep it and use it whenever he needs it as long as it is not disruptive.

When a child is caught between two troubled adults they may think it is their fault, that they are responsible and that somehow they need to try and do something to make it better. They may become preoccupied with this and have little or no time or space to engage with their learning or to develop friendships. Sometimes a child is constantly trying to repair their parents' relationship by their behaviour; for example, 'If I clean the house then Mum will be happy and won't shout at Dad when he comes home from the pub and tell him to move out.' This may result in them appearing disinterested at school as they are thinking of new ways to make things better at home. This behaviour may serve as a self-fulfilling prophecy for their internal script that is already telling them they are wrong and bad and things are their fault.

Staff strategy – focus on the behaviour you would like to see

Use positive praise posters on the wall around the class or on the door for other staff to see. Identify a child's positive behaviour and encourage children to contribute the examples of behaviour they see, and write them on the posters; e.g. John has been thoughtful today by helping Sunita find her lunchbox.

Relational experiences within the family

The ideas discussed in Chapter Two, which explores the impact of the family on the child's ability to learn and succeed at school, examine in more detail the effect of these experiences on children. If a child's needs are considered and met consistently during childhood they have a different experience to a child who has not had this. If a child feels unconditionally loved and valued for who they are and the joy they bring to their parents/carers, it is easier for them to approach and cope with school life. If a child feels that they are loved conditionally depending on their behaviour, or not at all because of their behaviour, their sense of being worthwhile, valued and bringing joy to other people may be an unfamiliar concept to them. As discussed previously, children initially develop core beliefs and ideas about themselves within the family and these are validated by the messages they receive about themselves, as shown in Table 5.1.

Table 5.1 Development of core beliefs within the family

Core belief	Validated by
I'm not good enough	Frequent criticism
My needs don't matter	Parent's needs always coming first
I'm not safe	Unpredictable and inconsistent parenting
I'm a bad person	Experiencing abuse/domestic violence

Some families may find it difficult to model positive relationships with each other or with people outside the family. As the family is the child's first classroom, the concepts they learn and experiences of how relationships are made and sustained are of crucial importance. This can be a major conflict between home and school. When a child learns within the family that relationships are about power, control and manipulation, and are encouraged to fight verbally and physically to get their needs met, the school setting with its different set of relational expectations and rules can be a very confusing place. It is a challenge to encourage children to develop and implement the school's relationship system in a way that is not demonising or criticising the child's experience within their family. How do we manage this without giving the message that school is right and your family is wrong?

Case study

Carl, aged 9, witnessed his mum and dad hitting each other whenever they were angry, which was frequently. He learned and witnessed repeatedly that this is how to respond to conflict. The messages he received were that if someone says or does something that you do not like then you need to hit them. This was reinforced by his parents telling him he was soft if he didn't demonstrate this behaviour towards other children in the street.

At school Carl was very confused. If he behaved in a way that his parents approved of and that pleased them, then he received disapproval and got in trouble at school. He was constantly having to juggle two conflicting ways of behaving and would just be getting used to this when there was a school holiday and he would have to start all over again.

Relational templates

The relationships that are demonstrated between the adults within the child's family provide powerful experiences of how to manage those outside it. While children may not be able to differentiate between helpful and harmful responses to situations, they are reliant on adults to provide examples of this for them. The way that this is shown to children can either help or hinder their ability to build relationships themselves.

Reflect: What messages may be provided by the following situation?

A child witnesses their parents arguing and fighting. Mum tells Dad to leave and Mum gets a new boyfriend. Mum tries to stop Dad seeing the child as a way of punishing him. Dad refuses to give Mum any money until she lets him see the child and tries to phone the child to speak to them. Mum refuses to let the child speak to Dad or have any contact with him.

Messages to the child:

- Conflicts are not resolvable.
- Relationships are replaceable (mum gets new boyfriend).
- Relationships are about power and control.
- Relationships are not about compromise or negotiation.
- Relationships are confusing and unpredictable.
- My thoughts and feelings don't matter.

Children bring their templates of how to build and maintain relationships with them in to school. Each child already has countless examples of relationships they have experienced and witnessed by the time they come to school and their experiences at school can either reaffirm or challenge this.

Negative messages children may learn about relationships within the family:

- You have to fight for everything.
- Relationships are hard.
- Don't trust anyone.
- Everyone is out to get you.
- It's good to get one over on people.
- Having feelings is a weakness.
- It's good to hurt other people.
- Don't be vulnerable.

Within the family there are expectations that parents love each other and their children, but this can be difficult to do if a parent has not had this experience themselves and does not understand how to do this. The experience of how sibling relationships are established and managed within the family provides a useful opportunity for families to encourage children to practise and develop skills that will be beneficial at school and in the wider community. When children have had positive experiences of managing feelings of jealousy with siblings, along with dealing with conflict and competition in a positive way, this enables them to transfer these skills to experiences at school. The relational patterns that children are exposed to are internalised and may become a reality in school. Children develop their own internal guide to making friends and engaging in relationships with adults in school and this may manifest in their behaviour towards other people (see Table 5.2).

Table 5.2 What has this child been taught in their family?

Kindness	or	Hostility
Compassion		Humiliation
Respect		Degradation
Understanding		Hostility
Tolerance		Indifference
Acceptance		Rejection

Helping children to develop appropriate friendships

When children have had the experiences described, it is important that the school recognises that they may not have the social and emotional skills appropriate for their age. It is vital that each child is assessed for this rather than expecting them to automatically be able to manage relationships with children and school staff. It is crucial that they support children who do not have the skills to build and maintain friendships, rather than punish them for not having them.

The school setting provides the ideal situation for children to learn basic friendship skills and it is useful to explore opportunities within the school day and at after school activities to do this. Children who have friends feel happy, confident and good about themselves. They are more able to focus and engage with their learning rather than feeling worried and anxious about their lack of friends and how they feel about themselves. The school can support children who need additional help to build friendship skills by using a caring approach that is nurturing rather than punitive, which will achieve more positive results.

The group work programmes provide an opportunity for children to receive additional support with their social and emotional development which enables them to develop the necessary skills to manage relationships more successfully. The activities and tasks are devised to enable children to practise social skills such as sharing, compromising, negotiating, waiting for their turn, etc., which are skills that some children may not have had the opportunity to develop outside school. The supportive environment created by the group facilitator enables children to experiment with behaving differently and taking a risk. For children who have no resilience, lack confidence and self-esteem, and can't manage their peer relationships, the chance to practise these skills in a safe and supportive environment can help eliminate their feelings of vulnerability and isolation. The group can encourage children to have good feelings about themselves by providing messages such as 'You can contribute your ideas and do things well, people like you', which are all essential ingredients to enable children to build and sustain friendships. The sense of belonging created by being in the group on a weekly basis enables children to build an alliance with the others in the group and assists them in building friendships that may be transferred outside the group.

The activities and tasks in the group work programmes enable children to develop positive feelings about themselves through their behaviour. For example, an activity making something for someone else (see page 105) provides an opportunity to explore how this feels and why. This develops positive feelings and increases the likelihood of the behaviour being repeated outside the group so children activate those feelings about themselves again. The development of these skills and the heightened awareness of other people enable friendship skills to be practised and implemented on a daily basis. For example, a child who was previously quiet and withdrawn may find his voice and start offering to help the class teacher more often. The benefits of the group work programmes are discussed in more detail in Chapter Seven.

Children who need help with friendships

There are a variety of reasons why some children find it more difficult to make friends and we have already explored some of these. When a child does not have the skills to make connections with other people they may use their behaviour as a way of getting a response and being noticed; for example, a child who pokes or prods another child to make a connection because they do not have the language or social skills to know where to begin. For children who find making and keeping friends difficult, it can reinforce their sense of loneliness and isolation when they can't seem to get it right in making connections with other children.

Case study

Katie, aged 10, was very unconfident and didn't know how to make or sustain friendships. She was very boisterous and would knock children over when playing with them and cry inconsolably when it was pointed out that she had hurt them. Her lack of resilience resulted in her being controlling and possessive on the rare occasions when the other children included her. Consequently the other children started to avoid her.

Katie's poor social skills, emotional vulnerability and challenging behaviour all resulted in her behaving at the developmental level of a child of a much younger age. The other children then started teasing her about this and calling her a baby. This downward spiral can be difficult to break without additional help, nurture and support in school.

Staff strategy – the 'book of kind things'

For children such as Katie, devise 'Katie's book of kind things' and find one kind thing every day that she can do to help staff, children or around the school generally. At first they may need help identifying what they can do, but gradually encourage them to have their own ideas. Each day record this in their book which they can decorate and keep in their drawer at school. Every Friday photocopy the week of kind things for them to take home.

This activity helps to identify positive aspects of the child and focuses on finding qualities they possess that may otherwise be overlooked due to their challenging behaviour. It builds their confidence and self-esteem as they start to feel better about themselves and realise what they have to offer. The responses from the other school staff and children help to support this and enable the child to be viewed in a more positive way. Gradually they are able to practise social skills once they feel more confident and have a stronger sense of self.

Reflect: Think of a child you know and consider the child's relational template

- What is this child's experience of relationships at home?
- What is this child's experience of relationships at school?
- What do they need?
- How can I help them with this?

Children who bully

Children who torment, intimidate, control or manipulate other children may be showing adults they desperately need help with their social and emotional skills. When a child displays any of these behaviours they are clearly communicating that they are unhappy and need help to feel better about themselves. Children who actively hurt others are often hurting themselves. Children who are happy and settled do not need to hurt other people.

Possible reasons for children bullying:

- low self-esteem;
- lack of confidence;
- negative sense of self such as 'I'm a bad person, I'm not good enough';
- being bullied themselves;
- being controlled outside school so using control to feel powerful;
- lack of control and choices at home.

While it may be a challenge for school staff to look beyond the child's behaviour, this is the key to enabling them to change it. Children who display bullying behaviour need nurturing and to feel good about themselves.

Children who bully need:

- opportunities to develop personal strengths and qualities;
- to have choices and contribute to decision making wherever possible;
- a positive relationship with an identified person who can get to know them and support them to get their needs met in more positive ways;
- school staff to show an interest in them and spend time getting to know them so they feel more positive about who they are.

Reflect: Dealing with bullies

- How does your school deal with children who bully?
- Does this activate more negative feelings and increase self-loathing for them?
- If so, how can this be changed?

Children who experienced multiple transitions

As mentioned in Chapter Two, children who have moved house and school several times in their lives may need extra support with friendships and adjusting to school life. They may require additional support settling in to the class and feeling comfortable at school. This can be achieved by providing additional adult help if it is available and preparing the class to welcome the newcomer. The experience of a new child starting in a class provides an ideal opportunity to work with the rest of the class to explore how this may feel and what they can do to help the child. It is a useful way to introduce concepts such as empathy, support, compassion, differences, etc. with the class and to enable them to practise and develop a new understanding and set of skills. The class teacher can consider the class environment and where the new child will sit, who can be a buddy to them and when and how this will be reviewed. If a new child is provided with a positive and welcoming start, this can help alleviate some anxieties the child may be feeling.

Children who experience many changes of school also need the opportunity to experience a positive ending from the school they are leaving, even if the staff are all breathing a sigh of relief.

This can be achieved by allocating some time with a familiar member of school staff such as a teaching assistant who can take the child on a tour of school, taking photos of them at various places such as the dining hall, playground, etc. and making a scrapbook with them. The rest of the class can spend this time making either individual or a whole class card for them to take with them when they leave. Give a child a positive ending at your school so they can have a more positive beginning at their new school.

Consider your contribution

The vast majority of adults who choose to work in schools like working with children and enjoy their company. The key to any good relationship including those between school staff and children is the ability to self-reflect. This involves an honest appraisal of the following:

● What do I react to and why?
● What do I struggle with and why?
● What do I honestly think about children who show challenging behaviour and why?
● What do I honestly think about children who bully and why?
● What do I think about children who lie and why?
● What do I think about children who steal and why?
● What do I think about children who hit other children and adults and why?
● Am I as happy as I could be with the relationships I have with the children?
● What could I do to change this?

The more honest that school staff can be with themselves about the behaviours and relationships that they find difficult and why, the more they are able to change this and improve the relationship they have with the children in their school. It may be a complex and painful task to do this, but it can also be a liberating experience resulting in staff ensuring they do not punish children for their behaviour because of how they are feeling. Some children may evoke difficult feelings in adults and school staff may start behaving differently towards them; for example, if a child has been rude or disrespectful towards you it may be hard not to ignore them or be stricter with them the next time you see them. It is essential that staff are able to separate the behaviour from the child and remember this is the way that the child is communicating; it is not a personal attack or a deliberate way of making your day more difficult. Explore what is motivating your response to a child and ensure you are responding in an adult way and are not locked in a power struggle with them.

If school staff are committed to having better relationships with children and are able to honestly reflect on the barriers that are preventing them from achieving this, then they have started on a journey to be able to achieve this. The following activity can be implemented using a class list every half term and is a useful way to keep evaluating your relationships with the children.

Reflect: How well do I know my class?

Look at your class list and consider the following:

● How well do I know the children in my class?
● How do I manage my relationships with quieter/shy/less confident children?
● Which children do I have good relationships with and why?

Staff experiences

Each member of school staff will have their own story and experience of their own schooling that they bring with them to work every day. This may have been a positive or negative event and may impact on their present day experiences in school. It may affect the way they interact with the children, their beliefs about behaviour and how it should be responded to, along with how they feel about their job.

Reflect: How does your experience of school impact on your relationships with children and reactions to their behaviour?

Think of a child who you find challenging or difficult.

- What is it that you find difficult?
- Do they challenge you or undermine you?
- How does that make you feel?
- Why do you think they do this?
- What can you do to improve your relationship with that child?
- How would you feel if you achieved this?

Both school staff and children will bring experiences and ideas to the school setting each day. Children bring their own experiences of how behaviour is managed at home and in the wider community, along with attitudes to school and learning and an acceptable code of conduct they have learned. Adults have their own experiences of early childhood programming that they carry with them into adulthood. School staff bring their own expectations about how behaviour should be managed, their own attitudes towards school and learning along with an acceptable code of conduct they have learned. The more compatible these are, the higher the likelihood of successful relational experiences occurring for staff and children.

Reflect: On your journey in to work each day ask yourself

- How do I feel?
- What am I bringing with me to school today?
- What can I do to ensure it doesn't have a negative impact on my relationships and my day?

The quality of the staff and child relationship

The quality of the staff and child relationship affects the teacher both emotionally and professionally and the child in terms of outcome, achievement and positive sense of self. The staff perception of the child affects the relationship between them and the staff's efforts to engage and motivate the child. There are some children that it is very easy for school staff to have a good relationship with. These children are often confident, articulate and pleasant to spend time with. They are compliant and respond well to adult interactions and praise. However, it is the children that staff find most challenging and difficult to spend time with who need it the most. These children may present as antagonistic, argumentative and disrespectful. They may appear to have no interest in building relationships with school staff and seem to go out of their way to make school life as hard as possible for themselves and everyone around them. It is not surprising therefore that most school staff would not choose to actively try and develop a relationship with them.

Staff strategy – to help a child who finds it hard with new members of staff

Work with the child to create a 'getting to know me' information sheet.
   Include:

- Things I would like you to know about me are ...
- You can help me by ...
- Please do ...
- Please don't ...

When a child has a support worker working with them on an individual basis, the relationship between them can be very intense. It is sometimes the children that most need help with relationships, either with children or adults, that have support workers and this can contribute to the need for extra help and guidance for the member of staff working in this role in school. They play a valuable part in ensuring that children are able to reach their full potential, but the role is not without its difficulties. For example, a child may find it hard to settle and engage when the support worker is not there or may be jealous or find it hard to share them with other children in the class and across the school. It is crucial that their role is clearly explained to both the child and worker to ensure that these situations are easier to deal with. The school can offer support for the child around these changes and provide them with explanations and advance warning. For example, a child could go to another class to work with a teacher they are familiar with if their support worker has to go to a meeting and they may find it difficult to manage their behaviour in class without them. This is a useful opportunity to make appropriate changes to meet the child's needs and is not rewarding the child for their behaviour. It is important this is explained to all school staff to ensure there is understanding across the staff team and to discuss why this change is being implemented.

Building relationships

It is worthwhile exploring what opportunities exist in school to build relationships between staff and children and how these can be increased. In the classroom there are situations that can be adapted to develop relationships more fully; for example, during wet play where children are unable to go outside, or free choice time known as 'golden time' in some schools. While it may be tempting to spend this time marking or doing preparation, it can be a good time to develop relationships with the children and to see other aspects of their personalities in an informal, relaxed and fun way.

   For some children, the experience of spending individual time with a member of school staff may seem terrifying. These children may have experienced adult relationships as being unpredictable and inconsistent and have developed this avoidance as a coping strategy and a way of feeling safe. They need to be able to experiment being in close proximity to an adult while still feeling safe and in control. A useful way to provide this can be to offer them the opportunity to choose a friend to do a job for you with them. This gives them permission to be as close or distant from you as they need to be. Gradually, over time as they develop a relationship with you, they may become more relaxed and be able to initiate this for themselves. It is essential that they are encouraged to build the relationship themselves and that it is not rushed as this may result in them feeling anxious and overwhelmed.

Staff strategy – have I encouraged the children I work with to feel good about themselves today?

● Have I praised them?
● Have I acknowledged positive behaviour?
● Have I identified helpful hands?
● Have I recognised both effort and achievement in children's work?

Staff leaving

When a member of school staff leaves the school either during or at the end of the school year, this can have a big impact on some children. It is important for schools to consider how this is communicated to the children and when they are told. Some children develop close relationships with school staff and are devastated when they leave. It can be a huge loss for them and needs to be managed with thought and sensitivity. Children need to be given plenty of notice rather than being told on the day the person is leaving. The ending needs to be marked in some way and the children offered the opportunity to make cards or draw pictures if they wish to. They need clear and honest explanations and the chance to ask questions in order to understand what is happening. When children have experienced adults coming in and out of their lives or just disappearing overnight due to relationship breakdown, it is essential that schools provide them with a supportive and reassuring experience of an ending with an adult.

How do children experience school staff?

As I discussed earlier in this chapter, each child brings their own template of relationships to school with them based on their experiences outside school. The relationships with staff at school can provide an alternative template for some children. For children who have developed vigilance as a way of feeling safe, they may notice non-verbal as well as verbal responses to situations. For example, does a member of staff frequently stand with their arms folded or regularly frown or look cross? What may this communicate to a child? In order for school staff to develop positive relationships they need to be aware of the significance of every interaction with children.

Reflect: How approachable are you?

● Do you smile at children when you see them?
● Do you show children you can be trusted?
● Do you show interest in the children?
● Do you encourage children to talk to you if they want to?
● Do you listen when children talk to you?
● Do you support children with their feelings?

The acknowledgement of your role in school can also help to support this process; for example, offering help to a child by saying 'Sometimes adults can help you with things' or 'My job is to keep you safe' to a child who is being bullied. These responses are particularly important for children who have learned self-sufficiency as a coping mechanism in order to feel safe. If staff listen to children's thoughts, ideas and opinions they feel listened to and valued and may be more inclined to repeat this behaviour. When school staff respond to children's anxieties and fears with compassion and understanding rather than dismissing them as silly or inconsequential, they are validating the child's experience and enabling them to feel safe and supported at school. In school, it is essential that staff take responsibility for and acknowledge their own mistakes and apologise when they get things wrong. We cannot expect children to do this if we are not able to do this as adults.

When children interrupt staff frequently and find it hard to wait to be listened to, this may be an indication they do not get heard at home. It is important to be aware of how children who interrupt are responded to in school: are they criticised or humiliated thereby evoking feelings of shame for the child, or responded to in an understanding way? It is very difficult for children (and some adults) to not say what comes into their head immediately. It is helpful and supportive to a child's confidence and self-esteem if they can be praised for being patient rather than penalised for being impatient.

During the group work programme I acknowledge a child interrupting by saying 'It's hard to wait when you have something you want to say, but try and remember it and I'll come back to you in a minute,' or I focus on their ability to be patient by saying 'Well done for being so patient – that can be a hard thing to do.' These responses support the child in trying to change their behaviour rather than a punitive response which may make them feel uncomfortable.

When children feel that their opinion matters it enables them to formulate their own ideas, to make decisions and to value what they think. This is essential for the development of confidence and self-esteem and to cultivate a strong sense of self-worth. When children are encouraged to have dreams and aspirations and these are responded to in a positive way by school staff it provides a message of hope and conveys that things are achievable. This motivational response can help children to believe that things are possible and work to achieve them.

What are staff modelling by their relationships with each other?

Throughout the school day staff are interacting with each other and working together or alongside each other. School staff are provided with endless opportunities to model positive ways of interacting and demonstrate harmonious working relationships. It is useful to consider the relationships between staff and the messages they provide to the children; for example, does a child think 'Miss Jones must hate Mrs Sullivan, she's always moaning about her'? This response is not only unprofessional and inappropriate for a child to witness, it also communicates about how to manage conflict, i.e. just moan rather than talk to the person and try and work out what the problem is. Adults working with children have a responsibility to demonstrate appropriate ways of expressing and dealing with their own feelings; for example, sharing excitement about a school trip.

What message does the following behaviour communicate to children?

- Staff being negative about each other.
- Staff snapping at each other.
- Staff challenging each other in an aggressive manner.
- Staff asking each other for help.
- Staff providing help to each other.
- Staff supporting and encouraging each other.
- Staff being relaxed with each other.
- Staff respecting each other.
- Staff valuing each other's opinions.
- Staff communicating easily and clearly to each other.

Reflect: Do staff walk their talk?

Do school staff behave as they expect the children to?

When children are trying to navigate their way around their life at home with unpredictable and inconsistent parenting they do not have a map to help them make sense of it. At school they are provided with a clear map in terms of rules and boundaries, but may need additional help understanding and following it. The school staff's increased awareness of this need for some children enables them to provide opportunities to support them with this throughout the school day. If children feel happy, safe, settled, valued and secure in school then with the support of school staff they are able to be focused and ready to learn. They have the capacity to reach their full potential. How many children in your school feel like this every day and what can you do to improve it?

6   You can make a difference

The vital role that school staff play in contributing to children's emotional well-being cannot be underestimated and can be utilised more to ensure it is maximised to its full capacity. Every adult who works in a school has a responsibility to support children's emotional health and well-being and contribute to ensuring they feel good about themselves on a daily basis. The quality of the relationship between adults and children is crucial and every interaction can have a positive and meaningful outcome. As I discussed in Chapter Five, everything you say and do can affect children in either a positive or negative way, it can either enhance or erode their self-esteem and sense of self. We need to consider carefully what we say and how we say it, as this can have a big impact on a child. Our facial expression, body language and tone of voice all have meaning and will be interpreted by the child who is on the receiving end. This is of vital importance for children who are tuned in to adults' every move. They can be vigilant at trying to translate every movement and gesture, as well as the actual words that are spoken. When children have had negative experiences of how adults perceive them, they are especially competent at looking for evidence to validate this negative view of themselves. Mannerisms such as an adult waving their arms around, even in excitement, can cause anxiety and increase stress levels for children who live with unpredictability. The use of a gentle tone can go a long way in establishing a safe relationship for a child who is anxious and scared.

Reflect: Think about the changes you can make

- What can I do to make a difference to a child in school today?
- Will this make a small difference to me but a big difference to a child?
- How committed am I to making a difference to a child's life?

Try alternative ways to respond to children's behaviour

Throughout this book I have been encouraging school staff to try different strategies to deal with children's behaviour. It can be easy in life to keep doing things the way we've always done them and harder to be brave enough to experiment with another way. However, as has been discussed in the previous chapters, the significant relationships between school staff and children that can occur in school settings enable both children and staff to experiment with this concept. The more that school staff can get to know and understand the children in their care, the more they will be able to develop appropriate responses to behaviour to meet the child's needs.

Case study

Natalie, aged 9, found it extremely difficult to focus and engage with her learning for any length of time. She was very talkative and would often distract the other children sitting near her.

Teacher response

Her class teacher understood that this was something that Natalie found difficult and needed help with so she provided positive responses to help her make changes to her behaviour. When Natalie was being loud in class she responded by saying 'Natalie, I can hear you over here. Well done for doing your work. I know you're reading the question out, but let's see if you can bring the volume down please.'

Result

Natalie responded to this nurturing and gentle response by smiling and getting on with her work.

While this teacher response may not have had the same effect with other children, if school staff are able to think for a minute before responding to behaviour, they may be able to adapt their responses to meet the child's individual needs. This may result in the child feeling more understood and have a positive outcome for both staff and child.

Focus on behavioural expectations

Sometimes addressing the class as a whole or wondering aloud can be a useful way of supporting individual children to try and change their behaviour and can be less punitive than targeting individual children. For example, when the noise in the class is increasing it can be helpful to acknowledge this by saying 'It's quite noisy and I'm just trying to work out where the noise is coming from' or 'The volume has gone up again, can we all try and get the volume down again please.' Both suggestions are clearly communicating a behavioural expectation for the whole class and provide gentle ways of helping children to achieve this. The behavioural change can then be acknowledged and praised such as 'That's much better, well done for making the change I asked for.' When all children are clear about the behavioural expectations that school staff have of them, it may make it easier for them to work together and support one another in achieving this. The focus and validation of the behaviour that you would like to see, rather than the behaviour that you don't provides a positive reinforcement to all children. This is particularly important for children who have the opposite experience of this outside school, as they are able to achieve a level of success and sense of accomplishment in school, increasing the desire for them to repeat this behaviour.

Staff strategy – to help engage the whole class

'Who can I see that looks ready to listen? Who can I see that looks ready for learning?'

This strategy is a gentle way of reminding the class of a behavioural expectation you have of them giving you their attention when you ask for it.

Spend extra time with children

Investing just five minutes a day with a child can have a huge impact. I have encouraged school staff to do this at lunchtime while they are clearing up or setting out the class and it has provided children with a different experience of a staff relationship. The child can be involved in sharpening pencils or putting out books and it enables an informal interaction to take place and the relationship to develop. The message it gives to children is positive in terms of validating who they are. In previous chapters I have discussed the importance of this and how it can enable their internal dialogue to be rewritten; for example, 'If Mr Malik has chosen me to do an important job for him at lunchtime then maybe I am not a bad person.' The outcome for the child is beneficial in terms of relationship experience and developing confidence and self-esteem. The sense of purpose and importance developed by offering children the opportunity to help with jobs enables them to feel better about themselves. However, a note of caution is necessary to ensure that children do not feel they are only of value or importance when they are helping other people, so this needs to be considered when identifying children who may benefit from this additional input.

Reflect: What do I do?

- How often do I show interest in the children?
- Do I remember things they tell me?
- Do I remember to ask them about things they have told me?

Be a significant adult

One of the joys of working in schools can be the opportunity to build relationships in an informal manner with children. These snapshot conversations that take place on the corridor and give us an insight into children's lives are so important for our relationship building. It can be very difficult to retain any of this information, let alone remember to ask about it again. However, if we are able to do this it can have a huge impact. As adults we know how it feels if someone remembers to ask us about something we have shared with them; we feel listened to, understood and validated for being important and worth thinking about and remembering. Imagine how powerful this would feel to a child, especially a child who is not used to this happening and imagine how good it may make them feel. For a child who is not used to adults outside school showing them much interest, it can make them feel special and interesting if an adult in school asks them if their dog is better now or how their new baby brother is.

Reflect: Draw the path of your life

- On a large sheet of paper draw the path of your life from the age of five up to now.
- Include significant situations, events and people.
- Reflect on where and how the people influenced you.
- What did they say and do?
- How did they make you feel?
- Can you do that for a child at school now?

Provide positive messages to children

I am sure we can all remember significant people that have had an influence on our lives. They may have impacted on the way we think and view things or the choices we now make in our lives. When I was 10, I remember my class teacher taking me to the staffroom with her when she had her preparation time as I was too disruptive to be left in the class without her. She used to draw lines in pencil to divide the lines in my book and I had to try and write underneath the bottom line to help me practise my handwriting which was very untidy. I remember feeling very important, pleased that she wanted to help me and determined to improve my handwriting. My writing changed significantly for the better that year because of the time and commitment my teacher gave me and the messages she provided about wanting to help me.

Staff strategy – choose a child

Choose a child you feel would benefit from some extra adult input in their lives. Choose one thing you could do each day for a week to provide a positive message to them. You can use ideas from the list below or think of your own alternatives:

- Ask how their day is going.
- Ask them if they would like to help you do a job with their friend.
- Acknowledge something positive about them.
- Remember something about them and share it with them.
- Ask something about them.

Don't underestimate the crucial role you can play in changing a child's experience of life and relationships. It may not be noticeable immediately or measurable straightaway but you never know what seeds you have planted or when they will grow. All school staff have a responsibility to invest time, thought, energy and commitment into exploring how they can contribute to and enhance children's emotional well-being on a daily basis. Every member of school staff has a role to play in helping children reach their full potential. You have to believe you can make a difference and start making it today.

Think of Jim

From 0–10 years Jim hears what a bad person he is at home every day. His behaviour at school is challenging and disruptive. The school staff find it hard to manage his behaviour and unconsciously reinforce the messages he has received at home that he is a bad person.

From 10–20 years Jim struggles with friendships and relationships and is often in trouble with the police.

From 20–30 years Jim criticises and struggles to manage his own children's behaviour and to have a good relationship with them.

From 30–40 years Jim's children don't want to see him and he is drinking heavily to drown out the internal voice that keeps telling him he's a bad person.

- Imagine if at age 10 Jim had been a pupil at your school.
- Imagine if he had been flooded with messages that told him he was a good person.
- Imagine if he had experienced the school staff showing him he was a worthwhile person who had good qualities to share with the world.
- Imagine if he had taken that confidence and self-esteem and positive sense of himself with him when he left the school.
- Imagine what his life could have been like at age 20, 30 or 40.
- Imagine if he had been lucky enough to come to your school.

Making schools happier places

Reflect: Stop for a minute

Ask yourself the following questions:

- Why did I want to work in a school?
- What did I want to achieve?
- Have I achieved this?
- What can I do tomorrow to make the school a happier place for the children?

In order to make a school a happier place for the children, parents and staff who use it, every member of school staff could contribute one small thing every day. This can contribute to changing the atmosphere and ethos of the school and is achievable by everyone showing a commitment. The quality of the relationships between children, parents and staff can change by smiling as you walk around the school. I work in several different schools during the week and certainly do not know the names of all the children and parents, but I smile at them as I walk around the school. I acknowledge children if they hold open a door for me (which they do frequently), by saying 'Thanks for holding the door open for me, that's very kind of you,' or 'That's thoughtful of you.' This enables the child to know that I not only appreciate them holding the door, but I also experience them as being kind or thoughtful. How often do we see children showing us kind, caring, thoughtful behaviour in school but choose not to acknowledge it or are too busy to do so? Let's commit to changing this and providing children with positive feelings about who they are and what they do as often as we can during each school day. If we believe in children, we enable them to believe in themselves.

Every child has the right to be happy, settled and achieving their full potential in school; is this true for every child in your school? If not, is there anything you can do to make a difference?

Part Two: Practice

Using group work to promote emotional health and well-being and manage children's behaviour

7 The benefits of group work

The second section of this book explores the group work programmes that involve a focused approach to help children to deal with many of the issues discussed in the first section of the book. The group work sessions provide a safe and structured environment that enables children to practise and develop new skills. The friendship group supports children who require additional support in developing and sustaining friendships, managing relationships, and dealing with conflict. The self-esteem group supports children who require additional support to develop confidence and self-esteem. Children can develop both sets of skills from participating in either programme, and they also contribute to the development of resilience. The group work programme in this book is carefully structured and the activities are clear, simple and easy to follow because the focus is on the relationships within the group and enabling children to make changes in their behaviour.

The rules for the group are negotiated and agreed with the children at the start of the first week and are revisited at the start of every session. This is discussed in more detail in Chapter Eight. The children are encouraged to decide the rules and contribute the ideas themselves, providing an opportunity for them to be listened to and valued for their opinion as well as being able to learn about choices, consequences and responsibility. The rules can be added to each week as the children become more confident and take ownership of the group. The group facilitator can ensure that certain rules are introduced each week if they will support the development of new skills for the children, for example, introducing the idea of being patient if the children are finding this difficult to do. The exploratory manner used by the facilitator to introduce this idea enables a discussion to take place about the meaning of the word and how the group can use it. This child-focused approach may result in a clearer understanding and more willing implementation from the children.

Opportunity to change behaviour

The experience of being part of a small group in a safe and supportive environment provides children with the opportunity to experiment with alternative ways of behaving if they so wish. The group facilitator encourages this process by offering praise and encouragement, along with acknowledging how difficult it can be to make changes.

Case study

Sally, aged 10, was excited to be in a friendship group and was very talkative and brimming with ideas for the group rules. A rule of 'listen to each other' was suggested by another group member, which Sally heartily agreed to but had difficulty following. She kept interrupting the other children which they found irritating.

Possible reasons for Sally's behaviour:

- She was the middle child of a family of seven children and had learned to interrupt to try to get heard.

● Mum had post natal depression following the birth of the last two children and was struggling to cope with the children and make time for them all.

The teaching assistant who was facilitating the group commented on Sally's struggle to follow the rule by saying 'It seems that you have so much to say it's really hard for you to follow that rule, but remember we will all have time to talk in here.' This reflection acknowledged the difficulty she was having and encouraged her to try and practise her listening skills within the group. Sally was able to stop her 'notice me' behaviour and wait for her turn as she developed trust in the facilitator giving her time. This enabled Sally to use the experience of being in the group as an opportunity to practise changing a behaviour that she found difficult. She gradually learned to adapt her behaviour and to transfer this to outside the group. At the end of the group work sessions her teacher commented that Sally was less disruptive in class and much better at waiting her turn.

The feedback and support provided by the other children in the group and the facilitator enabled Sally to receive feedback about a challenging aspect of her behaviour and to experiment with a new behaviour in a safe environment. The facilitator was able to see and acknowledge her progress each week and comment 'I can see that you are working really hard to change that behaviour.' This encouraged Sally to persevere and make positive changes to her behaviour.

The experience of being in the small group enabled her to practise and become competent at adjusting to an expectation of school and society in general, i.e. listening to others. The predictable format of the sessions provided her with a sense of stability that enabled her to feel safe to experiment making changes within the group. The facilitator's encouragement and understanding of Sally's behaviour helped to connect rather than separate them as they worked alongside each other to facilitate this change. She was able to develop self-awareness and became more conscious of the impact of her behaviour on the other children in the group. This heightened self-awareness enabled her to work on changing aspects of her behaviour in a positive way. The opportunity to practise and develop self-regulation within the group setting increased the likelihood of it continuing outside the group.

The examples shown in Table 7.1 are taken from children who have experienced the group work programme.

Table 7.1 Impact of group work programme

Behaviour before the group	Behaviour after the group
Needing frequent adult approval	More confident and less demanding of adult attention
Copying other children's work	Working on their own
Not contributing ideas to class discussions	Happy to share their thoughts and ideas
Shouting out all the time	Able to wait their turn and be patient
Not wanting to show their work	Being proud to share their work
Being quiet and reserved	Speaking out and being more confident
Talking about themselves frequently	Developing positive friendships and interest in other people
Interrupting frequently	Able to wait their turn
Easily distracted and poor concentration	Improved concentration and attention span
Telling tales and lying about other children	More popular, no longer telling lies
Restless and fidgety	More settled and focused
Regular tantrums and angry outbursts	Calmer and happier in themselves

Belonging and ownership

The rules of the group are clear and devised with input from the children, enabling them to feel a sense of ownership and inclusion as they develop the social skills necessary for the group to function effectively. This sense of belonging and experience of having their voice heard is particularly important for children who may not have this experience at home or may feel marginalised in the rest of their school life. Some children may encounter feelings of loneliness, isolation and rejection both at home and at school and the chance to be part of something on a weekly basis may help with this. This sense of belonging and feeling that they have something of value to contribute may enable them to develop positive feelings about themselves, resulting in increased confidence and self-esteem.

Children want and need:

- to be accepted;
- to be valued;
- to feel they have something to offer;
- to feel good about themselves.

Consistency

The group is held at the same time on the same day and in the same place each week, for example, Monday 10–10.40 am in the resource room. This consistency and predictability can reduce anxiety levels for the children and help them to feel safer in school. The sessions are clearly structured with a beginning, middle and end activity each week. The focus on time, and acknowledging to the children when they have five minutes left if they are involved in making something, provides a sense of reliability as they know what will happen, rather than finishing abruptly, which can increase anxiety. The sessions start and end in a similar way each week with the main activity changing, enabling the children to adjust to being back in the group by providing them with something familiar. This structure and regularity is crucial to the group work programme and the sense of belonging that is developed by the children. It provides an opportunity to be able to respond to organisation and predictable routines, of which some of the children may not have much experience. This also helps them to feel secure and more settled in school, often resulting in them being able to manage the time outside the group more effectively.

The activities and sessions are planned and organised in a way that enables the children to practise new skills such as negotiating, planning and predicting. They discuss topics such as jealousy, individuality and differences, validating and affirming the feelings that may be evoked by these. Children can experience their peer reactions to the situations that occur in the group as a way of normalising their behaviour, with reflections and commentary from the facilitator. 'Joe looked a bit cross that Sunita went first, but remember that we all have a turn to go first in this group and it will be your turn next week, Joe.' The development of self-control is a process that lasts a lifetime and the more opportunities that children have to develop self-awareness with the support of a nurturing adult, the greater the likelihood of them developing the skills for themselves. All these skills are crucial factors in the development of resilience.

Choices and consequences

The sessions provide children with the opportunity to understand about choices and consequences and the impact of these on the others in the group, as well as themselves. They are encouraged to think about and share how they feel about positive comments made to themselves by the other members of the group, and the facilitator is encouraged to address negative comments or criticisms in an open and honest way.

For example, when carrying out the activity 'Making a friendship bug for each other' (see page 98), Joel, aged 8, responded by saying 'That doesn't even look like a leg Marcus, it's rubbish.' The facilitator reflected by saying 'It can feel really difficult when someone makes something for us and we are not happy with it or feel we would have liked it to be done differently.' She then explored with the whole group how that comment may have made Marcus feel and encouraged him to say how it felt hearing it. This was carried out in a sensitive way without shaming Joel and was used as an opportunity to increase the group's awareness of how the words we use may impact on other people. This enabled the children to gain an insight into their own feelings as well as those of others, resulting in them developing a more extensive emotional vocabulary, and an increased sensitivity towards each other. The development of understanding and compassion for others is a crucial part of children learning self-acceptance and self-compassion. The opportunity to experience this within an emotionally safe and nurturing small group environment increases their understanding and the likelihood of them implementing it outside the group setting.

Developing new skills

The activities enable the children to gain a sense of achievement and the focus is on the effort made and the process, rather than the end product. They are designed to help the children experience success and gain mastery through challenge and perseverance. This is supported by focused help from the group facilitator if needed. This development of new skills may be transferred outside the group where other tasks may be greeted with effort and determination, rather than helplessness and resignation to failure. The tasks are planned to promote the skills we want the children to develop. For example, putting them in pairs to make a friendship poster promotes the skills of listening, negotiation, cooperation and considering the wishes of others even though they may be different to their own (see page 93). The activities provide an opportunity for the facilitator to explore the skills the children think may be useful for them to use when they are working on the task along with introducing new vocabulary and discussing these concepts with them. For example, checking whether they understand what negotiate and compromise mean, how these skills can be used and what potential difficulties may arise from this.

Within both group work programmes the children are encouraged to practise the skills they are working on outside the group during the week. As part of the friendship programme they are asked to complete a task outside the group each week that is designed to extend their social skills and encourage them to take risks within the context of a supportive group. These tasks involve them practising friendship skills and are designed so they become more challenging each week. The tasks are then discussed at the start of the following session and the feelings evoked by these situations are openly acknowledged and reflected upon. This enables the children to implement their new skills and see the immediate results of this behaviour for themselves along with building their confidence and self-esteem. This is discussed more fully in Chapter Eleven.

Validating feelings

An important role of the facilitator is to validate feelings and through the activities acknowledge that all feelings are acceptable. For example, week five of the friendship group involves a story and discussion about jealousy and provides an opportunity for the facilitator to acknowledge that although this may be a difficult feeling, it is experienced by most people (see page 102). The activity enables the children to normalise their feelings and integrate them more easily.

The sessions are focused on sharing how things feel and the safe environment created by the facilitator enables children to discuss feelings in a more relaxed way and gradually share their own as they become more confident. However, while the sessions encourage the children to share their own thoughts and feelings, the children are also given permission not to do this if they feel uncomfortable. This is crucial in ensuring that children feel safe and comfortable within the sessions and are able to choose when and how they contribute.

The friendship programme involves an activity in week six where each child makes a box for another child in the group. This provides an ideal opportunity to explore how it feels to make something for someone else and what feelings it may activate. It enables a further discussion of other times when they may be able to do things for other people and the potential benefits of this. They are encouraged to thank each other for making the box and then share how it feels when someone thanks you for something you have done for them. This enables the development of new skills both personally and socially, as well as the opportunity to experience sharing feelings in a positive and welcoming environment. They are also developing a sense of personal responsibility as a result of being part of a group, but making individual choices about what they share and how they behave within the group. This can result in an increased awareness of themselves and how their behaviour and choices impact on other people. This may manifest itself in a positive way outside the group and the children may develop an increased awareness of themselves, resulting in a heightened awareness of other people. A member of school staff commented on this increased self-awareness in the children and said 'I know the children who have experienced the group work programmes because they start holding the doors open for other people around school.'

Building relationships

The experience of delivering group work provides the facilitator with the opportunity to focus on and get to know the children in a more relaxed way. It enables them to build a connection and get to know the children better. This can help the other adults in school to build a relationship with the children as they are able to share relevant strategies on how to do this. The building of strong relationships with children gives powerful messages to them that school staff will support them and help them with their behaviour if they need it.

Case study

Tyrone, aged 8, was very quiet and withdrawn in class; he got on with his work and answered questions when asked but never contributed to class discussions. His teacher felt that even though he'd been in his class for a term he still didn't really know him and hadn't built a relationship with him.

Possible reasons for Tyrone's behaviour:

- Dad had left during the last school holiday and he'd only seen him once since then.
- Mum was still trying to cope with the loss herself, along with looking after a new baby.

The learning mentor who facilitated a self-esteem group with Tyrone was able to share with his class teacher the strategies she had used to develop a relationship with him. These included reminding him that she would see him next week and making eye contact and smiling when she spoke to him. She also used his name frequently to ensure that she maintained a connection with him. This enabled Tyrone to feel safe because he knew when he would see her again and felt valued and important by her affirmative approach to him. His class teacher started implementing the techniques in class with Tyrone on a daily basis and ensured that he explained where he was going when he was out of the class and when he would be returning. He also focused on using Tyrone's name and positive body language with him in the same way that the group facilitator had suggested. The combination of all these changes resulted in Tyrone feeling more relaxed and less anxious, enabling him to contribute more in class and gradually build a relationship with his class teacher.

The group work opportunity also provides a chance for children who struggle with and/or actively avoid adult relationships to have a more intimate experience of this. This can feel safer and less intense as other children are present and the relationship can be developed gradually in a more diluted way. It enables staff to relate to the children in a more relaxed way, to enjoy their personality and get to know and acknowledge their qualities, as well as offering a high level of support and attention.

The learning mentor who had delivered a group with Tyrone noticed that he smiled at her on the corridor around school after the group had finished. After a few weeks he stopped her and said 'Miss, do you remember when we made the award certificates – I've still got mine at home.' The group experience had provided him with the confidence to practise and develop a new relationship and then choose whether to continue developing this after the group had finished. It can sometimes be easy for children like Tyrone to go unnoticed in class as they may not present challenging behaviour or disrupt the class. However, these children need help just as much as the children who are showing confrontational behaviour, often more so as they may be more easily overlooked.

Staff development

The school staff who deliver the groups are able to gain awareness of how they relate to the pupils and learn new skills to improve their relationships. They also increase their perception of how they communicate with children, along with a deeper understanding of children's emotional and social development; e.g. Kathy was a very skilled teaching assistant who was good at building relationships with the children. However, she admitted that she sometimes struggled with developing and maintaining boundaries with the children, especially around finishing time if they were enjoying doing something. Her activities in class often ran over and she acknowledged that her time management was poor.

The experience of delivering the group work enabled her to practise new ways of working and to practise working to the times allocated for the activities. The five-minute warning she gave to the group before they finished the main activity allowed her to see that the children were happy with this as long as they knew what was happening and why. It enabled her to gain a better understanding of some of the emotional reactions and behaviour she had experienced from children in the past when she had expected them to just stop what they were doing. She transferred this time warning to the activities she carried out in class and was pleased to experience the results from the children being the same, along with helping her to improve an aspect of her work.

Delivering the group work programme provides the facilitator with an ideal opportunity to develop new skills that can be transferred to their role outside the group. The heightened awareness of children's emotional needs and the use of reflective language can both be integrated into the facilitator's existing role in school in a way that promotes their confidence and enhances their contribution to the rest of the staff team.

Positive messages

The use of reflective language throughout the group work sessions provides the children with a very positive message about themselves as it communicates 'I can see you, I am trying to understand you, whatever you are thinking or feeling is ok, you are worth thinking about and I am interested in getting to know you' (see Figure 7.1). All these responses reinforce that the child is important as an individual in their own right and provides a clear sense of acceptance of who they are as a person. The programme promotes an awareness of the children's own emotions along with sensitivity to the emotions of other people, resulting in an increased ability to put those feelings into words. The experience of the group work programmes and the facilitator's reflections given to the children are positive and powerful and for some children may provide new opportunities for them to be experienced in this way. The facilitator's use of reflective language enables the children to feel seen, heard, valued and understood – all essential ingredients to build their confidence and self-esteem.

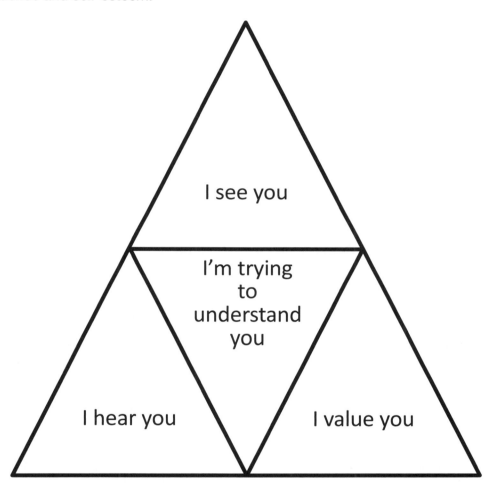

Figure 7.1 Positive messages to children

Communication skills

The group work provides an opportunity to develop children's social and communication skills and enables some children to find their voice for the first time, while others can practise being less domineering towards other people. For example, Louise, aged 10, was referred to the group by her class teacher who found her very difficult to have in class as she was constantly talking, interrupting and calling out. This was impacting on her learning and her friendships as the other children in the class were irritated by her behaviour. Louise showed this behaviour through the first group work session, but with reflections such as 'I can see you really want to say something Louise but I'd like you to try and practise waiting quietly while I listen to Yusef, and then we can listen to you' or 'Well done for being patient, I know that's difficult.'

Louise was gradually able to wait for longer and by the fourth session was able to listen more to the other children in the group. As she knew she would have her turn eventually, this lessened her anxiety and enabled her to practise patience and self-regulation. I spoke to her class teacher and encouraged her to try this reflection with her in class and she was pleased with the results and found she was calling out far less than she had been before the group. The teacher also talked to her about interrupting other children and Louise had said to her 'You know, Miss, I didn't know I was doing it, but now I'm going to try not to.' This increased self-knowledge and self-awareness resulted in a change in her behaviour and an increase in popularity with her peers in class.

New opportunities

There are children in our schools who have learned to hide themselves and their needs and instead have developed a way of being that puts everyone else's needs before their own. These children are often invisible in schools as their behaviour may not outwardly present as a concern, especially if there are a number of children who show their feelings in a more challenging way. The group work programmes provide an ideal opportunity for these otherwise invisible children to become more visible within the sessions and to start understanding and expressing their needs and wishes. There have been several examples of these children actively showing more confidence and having more of a presence in school. One teacher told me, 'He even walks differently now – I hadn't realised how much he was stooping until he started holding his head up high.'

The early messages some children receive about not being seen or heard may result in them finding it difficult to speak out in any situation and being quiet and withdrawn in an attempt not to draw attention to themselves. For these children the group work programmes provide an ideal opportunity for them to practise finding their voice and sharing their thoughts and feelings within a smaller group, if they wish to. As these children develop more confidence in speaking in front of their peers, these skills may then become transferable to the larger group within the classroom. The permissive and accepting environment created by the facilitator within the group sessions can enable children to feel noticed in a less threatening and exposed way than in a whole class situation. The reflective language used by the facilitator can enable the child to feel more confident at speaking out.

For example, Jonas, aged 9, was very quiet in class and his teacher described him as a child that was always eager to please. She described an experience of him offering to give another child his sticker he had earned for his chart, rather than putting it on his own. This made me wonder what early messages Jonas had received which had resulted in him believing that his needs didn't matter. In the group work sessions he was very quiet and waited until the other children had chosen the felt pen they wanted to use before choosing his. I encouraged the facilitator to offer the pens round the group the following week starting with Jonas and to acknowledge 'It's really important that we all have a chance to choose which colour pen we want to use.' The facilitator used this kind of reflection each week during the activities and gently encouraged Jonas to find his voice by reflecting, 'Sometimes we can think other people's ideas and suggestions are better than ours and that can make us not want to speak, but in here everyone's ideas are important.'

This experience may also benefit children who find it hard to make decisions for themselves. When adults are always in control and making choices for children, it is not surprising that children may present as helpless and unable to do this. The opportunities created by the group work experience enable children to make choices and decisions by the activities that are included, along with encouraging each child to have a voice and share their thoughts and ideas. For example, making a poster about themselves (see page 108), enables children to choose what they would like to include and how they want to share it with the rest of the group. If a child finds this hard they are provided with additional reassurance and acknowledgement of their feelings by the group facilitator.

The group work experience introduces many new ideas and concepts to the children. Along with the development of social and emotional skills, it can also expand the children's vocabulary by introducing new words in the context of the sessions. Alana, aged 9, was writing her name poem (see page 113) and was struggling to think of three words beginning with 'A' to describe herself. Her teacher and mum both described her as a chatterbox who never stopped talking. Alana wondered how she could use this and I explored with her whether she knew what articulate meant as I felt this was an appropriate word to describe her. She liked the thought of using it and told me proudly the following week that she had used it in her independent writing in class. The introduction of this word to her not only enabled her to view herself in a more positive light, it also increased her vocabulary.

Affirmative responses

Throughout the facilitator's notes I suggest reflecting 'You may need some help from an adult with this, and I can help you if you would like me to.' This reflection provides the message that sometimes children need help from an adult and it is acceptable to ask for it. This is particularly important for children who have learned self-sufficiency at a young age and will struggle on their own as they have learned 'It's not ok to ask for help or even if you do no one helps you.' It enables the child to have the choice and decide whether they need help, rather than the adult controlling the situation and deciding for them. I encourage the facilitator to say 'help from an adult' as a generic term rather than 'help from me' as this reinforces that other adults outside the group may also be able to help if they need it and gives the message that it's acceptable to ask them.

Positive changes in children

The benefits to the children of being in the group work sessions can become apparent to the facilitators as the sessions progress. They may see changes such as increased confidence, more willingness to speak out, being able to be patient while others speak. The class teachers have commented on improved concentration, improved peer relationships, more ability to recognise, express and manage their feelings, and more empathy with others. Some children have identified and shared the benefits themselves such as 'I like coming to school now', 'I've got more friends', and 'I'm doing better at my work'. Some parents have also noticed the differences in their children since being in the group work sessions and have said 'He's much happier in himself now,' 'He's getting on much better with his brother' and 'She's much calmer and can tell me if she's upset now.' These are examples of the visible impact; there may be many more that are less visible and that may only be noticed in specific situations – for example, less anxious about tests and more able to cope with losing.

The overall experience of being part of the group can not only be beneficial for school staff and individual children, but it can also highlight areas of concern and need for children that may otherwise be unnoticed. This provides the school with the opportunity to respond to this in a way that ensures they are meeting each child's emotional and social needs and promoting a whole school approach to children's mental health and well-being.

8   The role of the group facilitator

The group facilitator can be a learning mentor, teaching assistant, support worker, family worker, or have another role within the school, who has a thorough understanding of children's social and emotional development and is confident at working with small groups. They need to be interested in developing new skills to manage children's behaviour, have a capacity for some self-reflection and a willingness to try using the reflective language skills described.

The groups are most effective when they are implemented following the clear time guidelines set out in the group work packs as this enables the sessions to be structured and organised. The format is deliberately prescriptive and enables the facilitator to be exploratory with the children. There is a resource list for each six-week programme and these must be ready at the start of each session before the children come in. It is useful to allocate an hour to the facilitator for each group to allow for time to set out resources and clear away, reflect on the session and write brief session notes at the end of the group. They will also need some time to be allocated at the end of each six-week group to write a brief report on each child. This is discussed in more detail later in the chapter.

Completing questionnaires for the group

In order to maximise the benefits of the group work experience for the children, it is useful to complete a questionnaire for each child at the start and end of the intervention (see pages 124–5). This enables any changes that children have made to be monitored, along with identifying children who may benefit from additional support. The questionnaires are in the resources section and can be photocopied for each child. They can be completed by the child's teacher or by a teaching assistant who knows the child well. It is important that the start and end questionnaires are completed by the same person wherever possible. There is more information on how to complete the questionnaires in the group work questionnaire guidelines sheet in the resources section (page 123).

Developing new relationships

The group work sessions provide the facilitator with an ideal opportunity to develop their relationship with the identified children and practise a new way of managing their behaviour by acknowledging and reflecting their feelings. For example, providing gentle reminders of the rules and acknowledging that it can be hard to remember new rules can be an effective way of supporting rather than penalising children. For example, Kai, aged 7, was absent on the second session and at the start of the third week kept calling out when other children were talking. I acknowledged that it was particularly hard for him to remember the rules as he had missed the session the previous week and wondered if the other children had any ideas for how they could help him with this. The rest of the group suggested going through the rules again to help them all remember, which was an effective way of supporting them all and helping Kai too.

At the start of each session, after setting out the folders and resources and ensuring the group rules are visible to each child, the children are collected from their class and brought to the room. This is an important part of the process and gives a message of caring and nurture to the children. The children can be excited, scared and anxious at the start of the sessions, particularly the first one when they are unsure what will be happening. It can be useful to acknowledge this to them, e.g. 'It may feel a bit strange coming out of class with me, but I will explain what we will be doing when we get to the room.' This can help to reduce any feelings of anxiety and fear. The use of reflections provides all the positive messages in Figure 8.1 to the children and can be a useful way to identify the impact of its use.

Figure 8.1 Positive impact of reflecting

Sharing information with other people

There may be opportunities to share relevant information with children's parents or carers if this is appropriate. For example, if a child is trying hard to change their behaviour or has made a positive contribution to the group it may be useful to share this with their parent. This information can be shared in order to highlight the effort the child is making and to enable the parent or carer to support this behaviour at home. The friendship programme includes tasks that can be implemented outside the group on a weekly basis and it may be helpful to share this with the parent or carer to provide a clearer understanding of the group and to give them the opportunity to support this process if they are willing.

It can also be useful to share relevant information with the children's class teacher on a weekly basis so they can follow the child's process. For example, sharing that a quiet child has spoken for the first time and how this occurred. If children appear to be responding to particular reflections it is useful to share these with the class teacher who may also choose to use a similar response to help a child. Other school staff including lunchtime organisers, teaching assistants and the head teacher may also benefit from receiving feedback on the changes a child is working on within the group, so they are able to support this and acknowledge it to the child if appropriate.

Identifying children who may benefit from further support

The group work programme may identify children who need further intervention or specific focused help with particular areas. The facilitator will need to share this information with a more senior member of staff within the school such as the SENCO (special educational needs coordinator) in order to build on the work of the group where necessary. This can also be highlighted on the group work report under the section on recommendations. It is also essential that any concerns, a child disclosing or child protection concerns are recorded and passed on to the relevant member of staff, in line with the school's child protection procedure.

Writing reports

At the end of the six-week group it is useful for the group facilitator to complete a report for each child. The format and a completed example of this are included in the resources section. The report provides a short summary of the child's experiences of being in the group and identifies any recommendations that may assist the child further. This may include support from within school or on occasion help from outside agencies such as a mental health team. The report should include any additional comments from school staff as the example demonstrates. A copy of the report can be given to the allocated person in your school e.g. SENCO, head teacher, etc., along with the child's start and end of intervention questionnaires.

9 Starting and ending group work

The groups work well with a maximum of four children all from the same year group and preferably the same class to ensure the maximum impact of transferable skills on their return to class. They can also be delivered with a pair of children to provide a more intense and focused intervention, which can be useful for children who need extra support with sharing, waiting their turn and other social and emotional skills. This enables them to achieve success within a more realistic environment, which can then encourage them to practise these skills outside the group on a weekly basis.

Group composition

The group should consist of either all the same gender or an equal mix of girls and boys. This can be particularly beneficial for Year 5 and 6 children where they may become more aware of the differences between them and could benefit from extra support with managing these relationships. It is also useful to consider the developmental levels of the children that are to be in the same group to ensure that they will be able to manage the tasks at a similar pace and level. The personalities of the children can be considered too so there are combinations of dominant and less dominant children who can all be provided with support to make changes with their behaviour. Children can participate in both of the group work programmes, but this would be most effective if there was a period of time in between to integrate the skills they have learned.

When considering the group composition it is essential to consider each child's individual needs to ensure the group's success and the children's emotional safety. It is aimed at children who are low level disrupters and children who would benefit from additional focused support, rather than children who have more complex needs and may require more specialised intervention. If a child presents with very challenging behaviour and has complex needs then being in a group may be too intense and overwhelming, resulting in the child sabotaging the group as a way of managing their feelings. For these children, the activities can be delivered with one other child who has been identified as a role model, so the facilitator is able to provide more focused support. This may enable them to practise different ways of behaving and have this modelled for them in a nurturing environment.

Children who may benefit from the group work programme include:

- children who lack confidence or have low self-esteem;
- children who find it hard to make and keep friends;
- children who are quiet and withdrawn;
- children who are pleasers and feel their own needs are not important;
- children who interrupt and find it hard to listen;
- children who find it hard to share and take turns;

- children who tell lies;
- children who find it unacceptable to make mistakes;
- children who have regular conflict with other children;
- children who bully others or who are bullied themselves;
- children who are restless and find it hard to concentrate;
- children who are anxious, worried or fearful;
- children who lack resilience;
- children who lack self-awareness;
- children who are experiencing changes at home such as a new baby, etc.

The group is an ideal opportunity to boost children who are not as happy or settled as they could be or achieving their full potential.

Format of the sessions

The sessions are held for forty minutes once a week for six weeks. As mentioned in previous chapters, it is an essential part of the process that it is held at the same time, same day and in the same room each week as this models consistency and predictability, and provides structure to the children's week. The room must be available each week and have a table and chairs for everyone. Ideally this can be a small room where there may be minimal external distractions to enable the children to focus on the group. It is *essential* that the group is not disturbed by other people who need resources from the room or wish to use it as this can be very disruptive and gives a message that the group is not important. A sign on the door at the start of the session (see resources section) and a reminder at staff meetings can ensure there are no interruptions.

The room needs to convey a positive and welcoming message to the children as they enter it. The physical and emotional environment that is being provided by the group work is crucial to its success and impact. For some children, whose lives outside school may be chaotic and unpredictable, the calm, tidy and peaceful environment will enable them to feel safe and to settle more easily. They may be more aware of their physical and emotional environment and therefore the group work setting can provide an opportunity to relax and enjoy their time in the group.

Starting something new can make some children feel very anxious and scared. It is important that this is acknowledged by the facilitator (see page 94 for reflections to use). If a child looks anxious or uncertain it may be due to hyper vigilance and it is crucial that this is acknowledged. If the facilitator reflects on this and notices what the child is doing, e.g. 'I can see you looking at all the collage materials, maybe you're wondering what we are going to do in here today. I'll tell you when everyone has sat down.' This provides a strong message of acknowledgement and validation to the child, along with reassuring them.

When the children have all sat down in their spaces chosen by the facilitator, explain to them that this is a group that will meet every week for six weeks in the same room for forty minutes, and show them the start and end times on the clock. Explain that the group will meet at the same time and the same day each week and that if you are absent then they will not lose that session, it will be carried out the following week when you are back in school. Explain that the group will start and end in the same way each week and there will be a different activity in the middle. Discuss that the group is a way of helping them to practise and develop new skills, such as sharing and taking turns, and the activities will provide ways to help them with this. The facilitator's guidelines (see Chapters Eleven and Twelve) provide detailed step-by-step information for each session and it is useful to read these in advance of the sessions to ensure they are understood and can be followed easily. They provide clear explanations for the beginning, middle and end of each session, along with suggested reflections that may be helpful to use with the children.

On the first week each child is provided with a sticker with their name on it to wear for the session. This is to help the facilitator to get to know everyone and for the children to get to know each other if they are not in the same class. This is not necessary if the facilitator already knows the children and they are in the same class. During the main activity the children will sometimes be working in pairs. It is important that the children all have the opportunity to work with different people during these tasks as this will help them to develop new friendships and skills.

The facilitator must ensure they follow the time guidelines set out in the group work pack as this will enable the group to run smoothly. At the end of the session acknowledge their hard work, tell them you will see them next week and walk them back to their class. The facilitator needs some time at the end of each session to complete the register and session detail sheet (see resources section). The session detail sheet will provide a brief overview of how the facilitator feels the session went and a few sentences on each child; for example, 'The children all enjoyed making the boxes and were much better at following the group rules this week. Amy helped Kai with his box and was very patient with him. She seems to be increasing in confidence and is contributing her ideas more.'

Each child will be given a folder of the same colour for them to keep the activities in. They will also have a session chart to colour which shows how many sessions they are having and provides a structured beginning to each week as they colour in the appropriate number chart (see resources section). If a child is absent then they colour in the session number they have missed on their return so everyone's chart is the same. They keep the session chart in their folder and these are set out for them on the table when they come to each session and can be in the same place each week depending on the format of the activity and the needs of the children. The group facilitator keeps the folders and their contents in a safe place until the last session when the children can take them home if they want to. As this is explained to the group at the start of the first session, most children are ok with this. If a child finds this difficult it may tell us something about their experience of trust and can be reflected to them, e.g. 'It seems that you're really not sure about me looking after your folder, maybe it's hard for you to leave it with me, but that's one of our rules and I will keep it safe for you.'

Each session starts and ends in a similar way each week with an activity in the middle. It is useful to show the children on the clock how long they will spend with you so they are aware of this and it helps them manage the time. They will become familiar with the structure of the sessions very quickly and the predictability provides them with a sense of security. At the start of the first session after they have coloured in their session chart and the facilitator has explained about the folders, encourage the group to think of some group rules they will follow. The facilitator will explain to them that they need to think of ways to make sure that everyone enjoys being in the group and can start them off by giving them an example such as 'Listen when other people are talking.' The group can add to the rules each week if they need to, but they only need a few to ensure the group runs smoothly.

The rules are written out by the facilitator on a large card and put on the wall where everyone can see them. They are displayed for each session and can be referred to as a way of managing behaviour within the group. For example, 'I can see you really want go first Jane, but remember one of our rules is that we take turns. When Joe has had his turn then it will be your go. I know it can feel hard but let's see if you are able to wait.' The facilitator may want to think of some rules beforehand if they think the children may struggle to identify their own or if there are children in the group who may need specific support such as sharing the equipment, for example.

Although it is beneficial if all the children participate in all the activities and contribute to the discussions, it is important that children are given the option not to share their thoughts and feelings if they do not feel comfortable. This needs to be explained to the children at the start of the group work sessions (see page 94 for more detail). Once the sessions have progressed and the children are familiar with the format and feel relaxed, they are usually happy to contribute, but having the choice not to can help them with this. This is a crucial aspect of responding to children's individual needs and ensuring we focus on helping them to feel safe and secure before we expect them to change their behaviour. For example, a child who has been referred to the group because they find it hard to speak in class, needs additional support along with feeling safe to develop the ability to do this.

Preparing for the group

In previous chapters I have discussed the importance of school staff using self-reflection as a tool to explore and monitor their own feelings. This is of particular value to the group facilitator and can be implemented by checking how they are feeling at the start and end of the session. It is good practice to have time to prepare the resources beforehand in a relaxed way rather than rushing around looking for them at the last minute. I encourage the facilitator to spend a few minutes sitting in the room when it is prepared, before going to collect the children. Schools are extremely busy places and I appreciate how difficult this may be, but it is worth doing in order that the group is delivered in the most effective way possible. I suggest looking through the facilitator's guidelines and having them and the session plan accessible so they can be referred to easily. The children are usually too involved in the activities to look at them but the facilitator can acknowledge this by saying 'These notes are to help me run our group well and I want to look at them to make sure I do it properly so we all have an enjoyable time.' If a facilitator forgets something or makes a mistake then this should be acknowledged to the group. I once forgot to put their session charts out and I acknowledged it by saying I had forgotten and acknowledging that 'even adults forget things and make mistakes sometimes'. It is important that as adults we are able to model this for children as it gives permission for them to admit to their mistakes more easily.

The facilitator's use of their own internal check can be useful to develop self-awareness and appreciation of the importance of the tone of voice, body language and facial expressions being used (see Figures 9.1 and 9.2). All of these will be communicating powerful messages to the children and are worth exploring and reflecting on afterwards. This can be useful to look at after the session when writing up the session notes; e.g. if a session was particularly challenging, first explore how you felt, were you hungry, tired and a bit distracted thinking about what you had to do after the session? As the group work is a focused programme with a small group of children, it can be intense and tiring. In order for it to run most effectively the facilitator should enjoy delivering the programme and look forward to its weekly occurrence, rather than dread it.

Facilitator feels:
tired and preoccupied

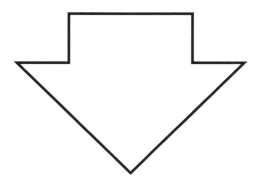

Child feels:
anxious and uncertain

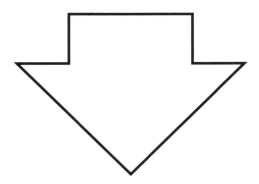

Group is:
disorganised and chaotic

Figure 9.1 Potential negative impact of facilitator

Facilitator feels:
organised and enthusiastic

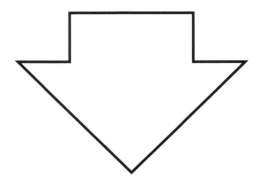

Child feels:
safe and relaxed

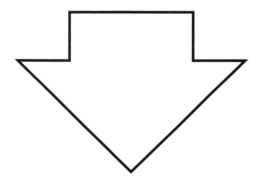

Group is:
productive and enjoyable

Figure 9.2 Potential positive impact of facilitator

The importance of endings

On the last session it is essential that the ending is acknowledged. For some children the group work opportunity has been the highlight of their week and it is important that the loss of the weekly sessions is given the appropriate validation. There may be children in the group who have experienced many changes and losses in their lives and these may not have been managed well, so it provides an opportunity for the group facilitator to provide them with a more positive experience. The ending of the group can be a good opportunity to validate the children's feelings about this and to be honest with them in a way that recognises and helps them manage their feelings.

The facilitator will start each session by stating the session number as the children are colouring in their session charts and acknowledge the remaining number of sessions. For example, 'It's our fourth session today so we have got two more sessions and then the sixth session will be our last one.' This provides the children with an opportunity to voice their feelings each week and provides the facilitator with insight into how each child manages endings. This information can be shared with the children's existing teacher to help them assist the child to manage changes that may occur in class and at the end of the school year. It can also be passed on to the child's new class teachers at the start of each year to enable them to manage the transition to their class in a way that meets the child's individual needs.

Case study

Grace, aged 10, stopped the group facilitator on the corridor regularly to check when the group was and whether it would definitely be running.

Possible reasons for this:

- Grace had moved school and home three times in her life.
- Her mum had had several partners; some who Grace had been attached to had left abruptly without saying goodbye.

The group facilitator was able to provide Grace with reassurance, acknowledge her feelings and ensure that she prepared her for the ending. She was also able to talk to her present class teacher to ensure that Grace was given advance warning of any changes wherever possible, and to work with her to prepare her for the transition to Year 6.

The opportunity for children to participate in an ending in a positive way and have their feelings about this acknowledged and validated is essential for their emotional well-being. During the last session the facilitator is encouraged to express their feelings about the ending and acknowledge that this may be difficult for the children. They are encouraged to respond positively to the children's expression of their own feelings about the ending in a way that validates and 'contains' them. This positive event may provide the children with a completely different ending compared to others they have had previously where people may just disappear overnight with no explanation being offered to them. This experience of endings provides them with a new template that is crucial for their emotional health.

10 'What ifs' for group work

The following reactions to events are rare and may never happen, but it is useful to be prepared for any responses you may experience:

- If a child doesn't want to come to a session check with the child whether there is a reason, reflect that 'It may feel a bit strange coming out of class' and encourage them to come: 'You can come and see what we are doing this week.' If they still choose not to come, then say 'We'll miss you and I'll come and get you again next week.'
- If a child comes to the session but is reluctant to join in, reflect that 'Maybe you are unsure about joining in today, you can just watch and see what we are going to do and join in when you feel like it.'
- If a child is disrupting the session, remind them of the ground rules and reflect that 'It can be hard following the rules but I'd really like you to …'
- If a child walks out of a session, remind them of the ground rules, encourage them to stay and reflect that 'Maybe you're unsure what we are going to do today; I wonder if it would help if you sat next to me?'
- If there are likely to be disruptions to the session by meetings taking place in the room or drums playing loudly nearby, ensure all staff are made aware beforehand that the room will be used, then acknowledge the noise from outside and reflect that 'It can be difficult to concentrate when there is a lot of noise outside.'
- If people walk in during the session, remind them you are doing the group and ask them to come back later; put a sign on the door (see resources section) and reflect that 'It's important that we're not disturbed because our time together is valuable.'
- If a child wants to take what they've made with them that week, reflect that 'You really want to take that with you today but you can take everything with you on the last week.'
- If a child shares something about themselves, e.g. 'I've not got a dad, I've just got a mum,' listen to the child and respond appropriately; if the child needs to talk more, offer to have some time with them outside the group where they can talk to you. Ensure you pass on any concerns to the relevant member of staff in school.
- If a child wants to give you their folder rather than take it with them, reflect that 'Maybe you want to leave me something to make sure I remember you, but I'll still see you around school and you can always come and talk to me if you'd like to.'
- If a child is absent on the last session, find the child when they are next in school, acknowledge that everyone missed them in the session and give them their folder.

11 Friendship programme and facilitator's guidelines

This chapter contains a weekly overview and facilitator's guidelines for each session. The weekly overview provides a summary of each week's session and activities. The facilitator's guidelines are more detailed and provide examples of reflections to use during the sessions. The group facilitator needs to take the facilitator's guidelines with them to each session.

The resources are in the resources section at the end of the book.

Overview: week one

Beginning (15 minutes)

- Introduce the group; explain about the time and number of sessions.
- Encourage each child to sit at the table, put their name sticker on (if applicable), colour their chart and write their name on their folder.
- Explain that you will look after their folder and that you will keep everything until the last session when they can take it with them if they want to.
- Explain that the group will start and end in the same way each week, but the activity in the middle will be different.
- Discuss the ground rules for the group, encourage them to contribute their ideas and write them up and display them.
- Explain that they will be given a task to do outside the group each week which they will be asked about the following week. Discuss the importance of their commitment to these and helping each other remember to do them.

Middle (20 minutes)

- Explain that they will be working in pairs making a poster about what makes a good friend.
- Explain that they can draw and write and encourage them to work together and share their ideas.
- Ask each pair to share their poster with the other pair and give positive feedback to each other; e.g. I like the picture of …
- Explain that as there is only one poster they need to decide how they will share it. If they struggle with this then the facilitator can suggest photocopying it or them having half each.

Ending (5 minutes)

- Explain that their task for this week is to talk to someone in school they already know and find out something new about them.

Facilitator's guide: week one

Beginning (15 minutes)

- If you already know the children and are not using the name stickers then indicate to the children where you would like them to sit.
- If you are using stickers put each child's name sticker out on the table, ensuring the children who will need the most support are sitting next to you.
- Encourage them to find their sticker and sit at the table.
- Reflect 'It may feel strange coming out of class with me today.'
- Reflect 'It may feel uncomfortable at first as we don't know each other very well yet, but we will spend the next six weeks getting to know each other better.'
- Discuss that the group is a way of helping them to practise and develop new skills such as sharing and taking turns and the activities will provide ways to help them with this.
- Explain that being in this group is a bit different to the rest of school because in here they can choose not to join in the discussions if they do not want to.
- Reflect 'It's really important that you feel happy being in here and sharing your ideas. Some children find this easy and other children find it difficult and that's because we are all different. It's ok in here if you need help with this and you can just say if you do not want to join in our discussions, but this group is to help make this easier for you to do this.'
- If a child is looking round the room then reflect 'I can see you are looking round the room, maybe it feels a bit strange coming in here.'
- Explain that you will see them every week for six weeks and if you need to miss a week due to a school trip or you being absent then they will have the session the following week so they will not miss the session.
- Tell them you will see them at the same time on the same day each week and show them on the clock the start and end time.
- Give each child a folder and a session chart.
- Encourage them to colour in week one on their chart and say they can choose which colour to use.
- Ask them to put the chart in their folder when they have finished.
- If a child needs help with this, reflect 'It can be difficult to do this and I wonder if you would like some help with it?'
- Explain that they can write their name however they want to on their folder as it is theirs and 'You can do it in big or small writing wherever you want to as it's your folder.'
- If a child looks unsure, reflect 'It seems like you're not sure where or how to write it, but remember you can choose and there's no right or wrong way.'
- Collect the folders and explain that you will look after them until next week and say 'When you come in next week I will have your folder and colour chart set out waiting for you, just like I did this week.'
- Introduce them to the idea of ground rules for the group and encourage each child to contribute if they wish to, allow children to just observe and not contribute if they want to, and reflect 'It can be hard to think of things to say so don't worry if you can't think of a rule today, we will look at this again next week.'
- Write the ground rules for the group on card and display them so all the children can see them easily.
- Explain that the rules will be up each week to help everyone to follow them.
- Explain about the weekly group task and reflect 'It may be hard to remember to do this, but we are a group and I will remind you if I see you around school and it would be kind if you could remind each other too.' Acknowledge 'It can be difficult to remember to do things sometimes and it is important that we all help each other with this.'

Middle (20 minutes)

- Explain that they will be making a poster in pairs about what makes a good friend.
- Explain that this will be their poster and they can decide together how they want to make it, they can write and draw if they want and you will help them with spellings if they need it. Reflect 'There is no right or wrong way of making your posters, the important thing is trying to work together and share your ideas and I can help you with this.'
- Encourage them to think about things they like and qualities their friends may have.
- Explore with them 'What do good friends do?'
- Encourage them to identify what skills they may need to use to work together and introduce concepts such as negotiating and compromising.
- Explore with them whether they know what these words mean, when it may be useful to use them and what may be difficult about using them.
- Encourage them to share their ideas in pairs and acknowledge 'It can be difficult to think of things' or 'Maybe you're not sure how to start but remember there is no right or wrong way of doing this, it's your poster and you can choose how you would like it to look.'
- While they are working on the posters encourage them to work together and ensure that all the children are contributing equally.
- If a child is taking over or not listening to the other child's ideas, reflect that 'I can hear you've got lots of good ideas, but remember we are working as a team so it's important that [child's name] shares their ideas too.'
- While they are working, reflect 'It can sometimes be difficult to work together on something as you may both have different ideas, but you are doing well at listening to each other/sharing ideas/working together.'
- If you notice a child looking at the other children's poster you can reflect 'I can see you looking at their poster and maybe you are comparing what you're doing on your poster; remember they will not be doing the same as you because you are all different people and may have different ways of doing things.'
- Try and spend time focusing equally on each poster, but don't offer praise or positive comments yet as this may influence what the other pair are doing on their poster.
- Tell them when they have five minutes and then one minute left so they are able to manage the time.
- When they have completed the posters ask them to share them with each other and give positive feedback to each other, e.g. 'I like the picture of them playing.'
- Praise them all for their hard work and comment on what you like about each poster.
- Encourage them to think about and name the skills they had to use to work in their teams, e.g. patience, listening, cooperation, taking turns, etc.
- Explain that as there is only one poster and two of them in each team they need to decide how they will share it in a way that is fair to both of them. If a child says the other child can have it then acknowledge 'That's very kind of you to offer but you both worked really hard on the poster so I would like you to try and think of a way that you could share it.'
- If they are finding it difficult to resolve this you can suggest photocopying it (do this after you have taken them back to class) or having half each so they are able to keep the poster.
- Ensure each child has a piece or a photocopy in their folder and remind them you will keep the folders until the last session when they can take them home.
- Reflect 'It can be hard when you've made something and want to take it with you today, but I'm going to keep all your things safe for you in your folder.'

Ending (5 minutes)

- Remind them that you mentioned the weekly task to be done outside the group each week and explain that you would like them to commit to doing these as you will talk about them at the start of each week.
- Explore with them what you mean by commitment and acknowledge that 'Everyone forgets things sometimes and you won't be in trouble if you forget, but we will all work harder to help you remember the next time.' This promotes a sense of belonging and group responsibility.
- Explain that the task for this week is to talk to someone in school they already know and to find out something new about them.
- Remind them you will ask them about this next week and reflect that 'It may feel a bit uncomfortable at first doing the tasks each week, but it can often feel like that when you are doing something for the first time.'
- Acknowledge that it is not always easy to do the task and ask them how they can help each other with this; e.g. reminding each other, helping each other if someone needs it.
- Praise them for their hard work in the session and tell them you will see them at the same time and in the same room next week.
- Walk them back to their class.

Overview: week two

Beginning (10 minutes)

- Encourage each child to colour their chart.
- Check whether they remember the ground rules and ask whether they want to add to them.
- Ask them about the task they carried out in the week and discuss how they felt about doing it.

Middle (25 minutes)

- Explain that you will be looking at making new friends this week and give each child the understanding differences interview.
- Put them in pairs and encourage them to do the interviews together, taking it in turns to ask the questions.
- Encourage each child to share how they felt about doing the interviews and asking the questions and discuss what they liked or didn't like about it.

Ending (5 minutes)

- Explain that the task for this week is for them to choose a child they have never played with before and spend some time getting to know them, remind them about the questions they have just been asking and suggest they can use these if they need to.

Facilitator's guide: week two

Beginning (10 minutes)

- Put each child's folder on the table in the same place as last week and put the ground rules up on the wall.
- Encourage them to find their folder and colour in their session chart.
- Acknowledge that you are pleased to see them all again.
- Encourage them to put their session chart in their folder.
- Show them the start and end time on the clock.
- Ask them if they can remember the ground rules and show them.
- Ask if anyone would like to add to the ground rules and remind them it's ok if they don't want to.
- Ask them if they all managed to do the task. If a child or children haven't done it then reflect 'Maybe it felt a bit uncomfortable doing it or maybe you just didn't remember. I wonder what we could do to help you to do the task for this week?'
- Ask the children who did the task how they felt about doing it, to share their examples, and whether it was something that felt ok or a bit difficult.
- Praise them for doing the task and remembering it.
- If a child has helped another child to remember, then acknowledge how thoughtful that child has been.

Middle (25 minutes)

- Explain that this week's activity is about making new friends and acknowledge that this isn't always an easy thing for people to do, so this will give them the opportunity to practise some things that may help them with this.
- Put them in pairs ensuring they are working with a different child to last week.
- Give each child the understanding differences interview sheet and offer them a choice of using a pen or pencil.
- Acknowledge that 'Sometimes we need help from an adult with things and I can help you with this if you would like me to.'
- If a child is unsure or you can see them looking at the pens and pencils to see what the other children have chosen, reflect 'Sometimes it can be hard making decisions, I can see you're looking to see what the other children have chosen, it's important that you choose what you would like to use, even if that is different to the rest of the group.'
- Encourage each pair to take turns interviewing each other and completing the sheet. They can do a question each or the whole sheet at a time, whichever they prefer.
- Acknowledge 'It's not a spelling test so ask me if you need help with this.'
- Acknowledge 'It may feel uncomfortable at first asking these questions, but this may get easier as you do more of them. Remember there are no right or wrong answers and you can choose what you say for the answer.'
- Give them permission to opt out of answering some of the questions by saying 'If you don't want to answer any of the questions then that's ok, you can just move on to the next one. We may talk about these afterwards so make sure you're happy with your answers being shared with everyone.'
- Try and spend equal time with each pair and help them with spellings if they need help.
- If you notice a child or children are finding it difficult or are unsure what to say, reflect 'Sometimes it can be hard to answer questions about ourselves.'
- They may need additional help with the last question, 'One thing my new friend could teach me is …'. You can encourage each child to think about what they are good at or like doing and see whether they could teach that to the other person.

- Tell them when they have five minutes and one minute left.
- When they have finished ask them how they felt about doing the interviews and asking the questions; you can start by asking what they liked or didn't like if they need prompting to get started.
- Encourage them to put their sheet in their folder and remind them you will keep their folder until the last week.
- Reflect 'It can be hard when you've made something and want to take it with you today, but I'm going to keep all your things safe for you in your folder.'

Ending (5 minutes)

- Explain that the task for this week is for them to choose a child they have never played with before and spend some time getting to know them; remind them about the questions they have just been asking and suggest they can use these if they need to.
- Acknowledge 'It may feel uncomfortable to do this and you may feel a bit scared at first, but I'd like you to try and do it, then we can talk about how it felt when we have our group next week.'
- Acknowledge that it is not always easy to do the task and ask them how they can help each other with this; e.g. reminding each other, helping each other if someone needs it.
- Praise them for their hard work in the session and tell them you will see them at the same time and in the same room next week.
- Walk them back to their class.

Overview: week three

Beginning (10 minutes)

- Encourage each child to colour their chart.
- Check whether they remember the ground rules and ask whether they want to add to them.
- Ask them about the task they carried out in the week and discuss how they felt about doing it.

Middle (25 minutes)

- Introduce the idea of making friendship bugs and explain that they will each add a part to each other's bug.
- Encourage them to think about the skills this activity will involve, e.g. cooperation, patience, etc.
- Give each child a piece of card and ask them to draw a head for their bug.
- Pass the bugs round and ask each child to add a body to the bug.
- Pass them round again and ask each child to add a leg to the bug.
- Pass them round again and ask each child to add another leg to the bug.
- Pass them round again so each child gets their own bug back and encourage them to add more legs or antennae, etc. if they wish.
- Ask each child to share how it felt making the bugs and how they feel about their own bug.

Ending (5 minutes)

- Explain that the task for this week involved cooperating and ask them to cooperate with someone this week and to bring their example to share with the group next week.

Facilitator's guide: week three

Beginning (10 minutes)

- Put each child's folder on the table in the same place as last week and put the ground rules up on the wall.
- Encourage them to find their folder and colour in their session chart. Acknowledge that you are pleased to see them all again.
- Encourage them to put their session chart in their folder.
- Show them the start and end time on the clock.
- Ask them if they can remember the ground rules and show them.
- Ask if anyone would like to add to the ground rules and remind them it's ok if they don't want to.
- Ask them if they all managed to do the task. If a child or children haven't done it then reflect 'Maybe it felt a bit uncomfortable doing it or maybe you just didn't remember. I wonder what we could do to help you to do the task for this week?'
- Ask the children who did the task how they felt about doing it, to share their examples and whether it was something that felt ok or a bit difficult.
- Explore with them how it felt to go up to someone they've never played with before, introduce new words such as embarrassing, awkward, etc. and ask if they know what they mean.
- Praise them for doing the task and acknowledge how brave they have been to try something new as this can be a frightening thing to do.

Middle (25 minutes)

- Explain that the task for this week is to make friendship bugs and encourage them to think about the skills they will need for this activity.
- Introduce the concepts of acceptance and tolerance and see whether they know what they mean.
- Explain that as each child will be adding a part to each person's bug and everyone in the group is different, they may find that they are not happy with the way someone else has done this, e.g. 'Mark you may look at the leg that Sara has drawn and think you could have drawn it better or not like the way she has drawn it, but being accepting and tolerant means that even though you may like it to be different you are able to accept it how it is and not make unkind comments about it.'
- Acknowledge that 'This is not an easy thing to do, but in here we are practising new ways of behaving and being tolerant of others is one way of us being able to do this.'
- Explain that it is different to being dishonest or lying as it involves being aware of how other people may feel when we say things to them.
- Remind the children to think about this when they are making a comment about how they feel about their own bug and acknowledge again that it can be hard to do this but you would like them all to try and do it.
- Give each child a piece of card and ask them to draw a head for their bug, pass the bug round and ask each child to draw a body for the bug.
- Pass them round again and ask each child to add a leg to the bug, and then pass them round again and ask each child to add another leg to the bug.
- Pass them round again so each child gets their own bug back and encourage them to add more legs or antennae, etc. if they wish.

- Ask each child to share how it felt making the bugs and how they feel about their own bug, reminding them to try and be thoughtful and kind when they are doing this.
- Praise them for being able to do this and acknowledge 'That can be a difficult task to do and you have all managed to be accepting and tolerant to each other.'
- Encourage them to put their bug in their folder and remind them you will keep their folders until the last week.
- Reflect 'It can be hard when you've made something and want to take it with you today, but I'm going to keep all your things safe for you in your folder.'

Ending (5 minutes)

- Explain that one of the skills the task today has involved them doing is cooperating, and check that they have understood what this means.
- Explain the task for this week is to cooperate with someone during the week and to bring their example to share with the group next week.
- Acknowledge that it is not always easy to do the task and ask them how they can help each other with this, e.g. reminding each other, helping each other if someone needs it.
- Praise them for their hard work in the session and tell them you will see them at the same time and in the same room next week.
- Walk them back to their class.

Overview: week four

Beginning (10 minutes)

- Encourage each child to colour their chart.
- Check whether they remember the ground rules and ask whether they want to add to them.
- Ask them about the task they carried out in the week and discuss how they felt about doing it.

Middle (25 minutes)

- Explain that this week's activity involves working together as a team and making one collage together as a group.
- Discuss how this can be quite hard as they may all have different ideas, etc.
- Give the group a piece of A3 card and a selection of collage materials and felt pens and encourage them to work together and make suggestions.
- When they have nearly finished the collage explain that as there is only one collage and four of them you would like them to decide as a group what they would like to do with the collage.
- When they have finished the collage ask each person to say what they liked and what (if anything) they found difficult about the activity.

Ending (5 minutes)

- Introduce the idea of feeling left out or jealous and explain that you will be looking at this next week. Ask them to bring an example of when they have felt like this to share with the group next week.

Facilitator's guide: week four

Beginning (10 minutes)

- Put each child's folder on the table in the same place as last week and put the ground rules up on the wall.
- Encourage them to find their folder and colour in their session chart.
- Acknowledge that you are pleased to see them all again.
- Encourage them to put their session chart in their folder.
- Show them the start and end time on the clock.
- Ask them if they can remember the ground rules and show them.
- Ask if anyone would like to add to the ground rules and remind them it's ok if they don't want to.
- Ask them if they all managed to do the task. If a child or children haven't done it then reflect 'Maybe it felt a bit uncomfortable doing it or maybe you just didn't remember. I wonder what we could do to help you to do the task for this week?'
- Ask the children who did the task how they felt about doing it, to share their examples and whether it was something that felt ok or a bit difficult.

Middle (25 minutes)

- Explain that this week's activity involves working together as a team and making one collage together as a group.
- Explain the task and acknowledge it may be a difficult thing for them to do as a group; e.g. 'Daniel may want you to do something about football as that's what he likes, but John may want to do a picture of the beach instead. I wonder what skills you will need to use to make sure that everyone feels happy and that everyone has been involved.'
- Encourage them to think of the skills they will need, e.g. cooperation, listening, taking turns, negotiating, compromising, etc.
- Explore with them what each word means and encourage them to start the task.
- Acknowledge each skill and praise them when they have used it; e.g. 'Well done Kiera, I know you really wanted to use the green pen first but you negotiated with Clare really well about how you could do this.'
- Give the group a piece of A3 card and a selection of collage materials and felt pens and encourage them to work together and make suggestions.
- Explain to them that as there is only one collage and four of them you would like them to decide as a group what they can do to make sure that it is fair for everyone. Try and encourage them to think of ways that are fair for everyone rather than 'Clare can have it'.
- If they suggest this or giving it to you then reflect 'Although that's a really kind idea, I'd really like you to see if there's a way that you can all have it.'
- If they are struggling to come up with ideas or reach a resolution, reflect 'It seems really hard for you to sort this out and I'm wondering whether you need some help from an adult? I wonder what we could do to make sure you all have a copy or a piece to take home as you've all worked hard on it?' You can colour photocopy it so they all have a copy or they can cut it into four pieces and each have a piece.
- Tell them when they have five minutes and then one minute left so they are able to manage the time.
- When they have finished the collage explore with them what they liked and what they found difficult about the activity.
- Remind them they can choose not to share if they do not want to.

- Acknowledge that the skills they have been practising can be difficult to learn and reflect 'Sometimes it can be hard working as a team and making sure you listen to each other and consider everyone's ideas, but you have all worked really well together.'
- Ensure each child has a piece or a photocopy in their folder and remind them they can take their folder home on the last week.
- Reflect 'It can be hard when you've made something and want to take it with you today, but I'm going to keep all your things safe for you in your folder.'

Ending (5 minutes)

- Acknowledge that you have been looking at different feelings in the group so far and that you will be looking at the idea of feeling left out or jealous in more detail next week.
- Explore with them what it means and ask them to bring an example of when they have felt like this to share with the group next week.
- Reflect 'It may feel a bit uncomfortable to admit that we feel jealous or left out, but everyone feels this sometimes and talking about it can help with those feelings. It's ok to feel like this and we're going to be looking at this more next week.'
- Acknowledge that it is not always easy to do the task and ask them how they can help each other with this; e.g. reminding each other, helping each other if someone needs it.
- Praise them for their hard work in the session and tell them you will see them at the same time and in the same room next week.
- Walk them back to their class.

Overview: week five

Beginning (10 minutes)

- Encourage each child to colour their chart.
- Check whether they remember the ground rules and ask whether they want to add to them.
- Ask them to share their experience of feeling left out or jealous.

Middle (25 minutes)

- Explain that you will be reading a story about feeling jealous and you will talk about it afterwards.
- Read the jealousy story to the group.
- Use the questions for discussion.
- Put the children into pairs and encourage them to think of a different ending for the story and act it out for the rest of the group.
- Encourage each pair to give feedback to the other pair after this and discuss how it felt to think of a different ending.

Ending (5 minutes)

- Put each child's name on a piece of paper, fold it over and give one to each child ensuring they don't get their own.
- Explain that the task for this week involves them writing a short letter or drawing a picture for the person they have been allocated and to bring it with them next week to give to that person.
- Give each child a piece of paper and envelope to use for the task.

Facilitator's guide: week five

Beginning (10 minutes)

- Put each child's folder on the table in the same place as last week and put the ground rules up on the wall.
- Encourage them to find their folder and colour in their session chart.
- Acknowledge that you are pleased to see them all again.
- Encourage them to put their session chart in their folder.
- Show them the start and end time on the clock.
- Ask them whether they can remember the ground rules and show them.
- Ask whether anyone would like to add to the ground rules and remind them it's ok if they don't want to.
- Ask them to share their experience of feeling left out or jealous and reflect 'Remember we said last week that it may feel uncomfortable to talk about this, but everyone feels like this sometimes.'
- Encourage each child to share but if a child looks uncomfortable or embarrassed Reflect 'I know it can be hard to share this but remember it's ok to feel like this and it can be good to talk about it.'
- Remind them they can choose not to share if they do not want to.
- If a child or children haven't done it then reflect 'Maybe it felt a bit uncomfortable doing it or maybe you just didn't remember. I wonder what we could do to help you to do the task for this week?'
- Ask the children who did the task how they felt about doing it, to share their examples and whether it was something that felt ok or a bit difficult.
- Acknowledge their work and praise them: 'Thank you for being open and honest and sharing how you felt; it's not always easy to do that, so well done.'

Middle (25 minutes)

- Explain that this week you will be reading a story about feeling jealous and that you will be talking about it afterwards.
- Ensure each child feels comfortable on their chair before you begin reading and explain that afterwards you will be thinking about some of the things that happened in the story and talking about them.
- Read the story 'Emily feels jealous' (see resources section).
- Go through each question, one at a time (see resources section), and encourage different children to answer without asking them directly but by being aware of any children that are not participating. Reflect 'Maybe some parts of the story remind you of how you feel sometimes and it may be difficult to think about when you've felt like that.'
- When you get to the last question about what they could do next time they feel like this, encourage them to identify their own solutions if possible, but prompt them if needed by saying 'I wonder if it might help to tell someone how you feel and I'm wondering who that person could be?'
- Put the children into pairs, and try and match the two more confident children of the group with the two that are less confident.
- Explain that you would like them to try and think of a different ending for the story and act it out to the group.

- If the children seem unsure about acting it out reflect 'You may be worried or embarrassed about doing this, but remember it doesn't matter if you forget what to say, I can help you with that.'
- If any children really do not want to act it out then they can just talk through the ending they have come up with and you can reflect 'Maybe that felt too frightening to do; you can just talk us through the ending you've chosen if that feels better for you.'
- Encourage each pair to give feedback to the other pair and encourage them to say what they thought was good about it or what they liked; e.g. 'I liked the way you got Emily to say it was her in the end.'
- Explore with them how it felt to write a different ending: 'Did it feel good to be able to think of their own ending?'
- Acknowledge their work by saying 'Feeling jealous can be a hard feeling to think about and you have all worked well on doing this today.'

Ending (5 minutes)

- Acknowledge that next week will be the last week and reflect 'It may feel a bit sad as we've worked together for a while and I've enjoyed getting to know you all a bit more than I did before we had our group.'
- Explain that you will give them all a piece of paper with another child's name on it and some paper and an envelope.
- Explain that the task involves them writing a short letter or drawing a picture for that person and they need to bring this to the group next week.
- Emphasise the importance of doing this task by saying 'It's really important that we all remember to do this task; how do you think you would feel if someone forgot to do one for you?'
- Acknowledge that it is not always easy to do the task and ask them how they can help each other with this; e.g. reminding each other, helping each other if someone needs it.
- Praise them for their hard work in the session and tell them you will see them at the same time and in the same room next week.
- Walk them back to their class.

Overview: week six

Beginning (10 minutes)

- Encourage each child to colour their chart.
- Check whether they remember the ground rules and ask whether they want to add to them.
- Ask each child to give their letter to the other child and open them.
- Encourage each child to say how they felt about doing and receiving the letter.
- Ask them to put their letter in their folder.

Middle (25 minutes)

- Recap each week and encourage them to remember the activities and tasks they have carried out.
- Give each child a box and ask them to write their name on it.
- Ask them to give it to the child sitting next to them and ask them to decorate it for them and give it back to them.
- Give each child three pieces of paper with the names of the other children from the group written on each one.
- Ask them to write what they liked about being in the group with that person on the paper.
- Ask each child to hold out their box while the other children put their paper in it.
- Encourage each child to read the comments they have received out to the rest of the group.
- Encourage each child to say how it felt doing this activity.

Ending (5 minutes)

- Give each child their folder and explain that they can take it with them if they would like to.
- Acknowledge how hard they have all worked and how much you have enjoyed spending time with them.

Facilitator's guide: week six

Beginning (10 minutes)

- Put each child's folder on the table in the same place as last week and put the ground rules up on the wall.
- Encourage them to find their folder and colour in their session chart.
- Acknowledge that you are pleased to see them all again.
- Encourage them to put their session chart in their folder.
- Show them the start and end time on the clock.
- Ask them whether they can remember the ground rules and show them.
- Ask whether anyone would like to add to the ground rules and remind them it's ok if they don't want to.
- Ask each child to give their letter to the other child and open it.
- If a child has not done the task then explore with them what they feel they need to say to the child they were supposed to be doing it for (this is unlikely as you will check with them all during the week to ensure they have completed it). Reflect 'I wonder what you need to say to [name of child] as I think I would feel upset and left out if it was me.'
- Explore with the group how they felt about doing the task and receiving the letter.

- Ask them to put their letter in their folder.
- Remind them that this is their last week and respond appropriately to any comments they make; e.g. 'I know it may feel sad as we've worked together for six weeks.'
- Recap each week and encourage them to remember the activities. You may want to have a list with you to help you to remember.
- While they are doing this you can acknowledge any memorable moments for you; e.g. 'I remember when you did the collage together and you all did so well working as part of a team.'
- Respond appropriately to any comments the children make about any memories they have by reflecting 'I hear you've got some good memories of our time together in the group too.'

Middle (25 minutes)

- Give each child a box, ask them to write their name on it and give it to the child sitting next to them to decorate.
- Remind them of the friendship bug activity and reflect 'Remember the friendship bug activity where you all did a part for someone else and we talked about how it may feel when someone else does something and it may not be the same as how we would do it; can anyone remember what skills we decided we would use to help us?'
- If no one can remember then remind them 'It was acceptance and tolerance; and why may we need to use those skills again with this activity?'
- While they are decorating the boxes explore with them how it feels to make something for someone else and the feelings it activates. For example, how does it feel when we do something kind?
- Encourage them to think of other situations where they may be able to do something kind for someone and explore how this may feel.
- Remind them they can choose not to share if they do not want to.
- Explore situations at home and at school where they may be able to do this and encourage them to do this during the week.
- Reflect 'Remember it can feel really good to do something kind or thoughtful for someone else.'
- When they have decorated the boxes, ask them to give them to the child whose name is on the box.
- Give each child three pieces of paper with the names of the other children in the group on them.
- Encourage them to think about each child they have worked with in the group and reflect 'Think about when you may have worked with them on an activity in pairs or with them in the whole group and what you've liked about being in the group with them. Remember it's not a spelling test, I can help you with any words you are unsure about.'
- Ask each child to hold up their box while the other children put the pieces of paper in.
- Encourage each child to read out the comments they have received to the rest of the group. If time is running out then ask each child to share one.
- If a child needs help with this then reflect 'Sometimes we need help from other people with reading and that's what I can help you with.'
- If a child is unsure or doesn't want to read theirs out you can offer to read it out for them and acknowledge 'Sometimes it's easier if other people read out things that have been written about us and that's what I can do.'
- Encourage each child to say how it felt to do this activity.
- If a child doesn't want to or looks uncomfortable, reflect 'I can see you're looking unsure about doing that and it's ok if you don't want to.'

Ending (5 minutes)

- Give each child their folder and box and explain that they can take it with them if they would like to.
- If a child doesn't want to take their folder or box reflect 'Maybe you're unsure about taking it back to class with you; you can collect it from the school reception area or office (depending on where is appropriate for your school) at home time if you would prefer to.'
- Acknowledge that 'Sometimes endings can feel sad and I have really enjoyed spending time with you all and you've all worked very hard in here. Although we won't have our group anymore we will still see each other around school, which I know won't be the same, but you can always come and talk to me if you want to.'
- Walk them back to class.

12 Self-esteem programme and facilitator's guidelines

This chapter contains a weekly overview and facilitator's guidelines for each session. The weekly overview provides a summary of each week's session and activities. The facilitator's guidelines are more detailed and provide examples of reflections to use during the sessions. The group facilitator needs to take the facilitator's guidelines with them to each session.

The resources are in the resources section at the end of the book.

Overview: week one

Beginning (15 minutes)

- Introduce the group; explain about the time and number of sessions.
- Encourage each child to sit at the table, put their name sticker on (if applicable), colour their chart and write their name on their folder.
- Explain that you will look after their folder and explain that you will keep everything until the last session when they can take it with them if they want to.
- Explain that the group will start and end in the same way each week, but the activity in the middle will be different.
- Discuss the ground rules for the group, encourage them to contribute their ideas and write them up and display them.

Middle (20 minutes)

- Explain that they will be doing an individual poster 'all about me' and they can write or draw things about themselves and their likes and dislikes.
- Ask each child to share their poster with the group and encourage them to look at the similarities and differences.
- Use this discussion as an opportunity to explore differences between people being positive, and introduce the importance of uniqueness.
- Ask each child to comment on how it felt to share their poster with the group.

Ending (5 minutes)

- Explain that the session will end the same way each week by asking them to share something about themselves. Go round the group and ask each child to say one thing they like.

Facilitator's guide: week one

Beginning (15 minutes)

- If you already know the children and are not using the name stickers then indicate to the children where you would like them to sit.
- If you are using the stickers put each child's name sticker out on the table, ensuring the children who will need the most support are sat next to you.
- Encourage them to find their sticker and sit at the table.
- Reflect 'It may feel strange coming out of class with me today.'
- Reflect 'It may feel uncomfortable at first as we don't know each other very well yet, but we will spend the next six weeks getting to know each other better.'
- Discuss that the group is a way of helping them to practise and develop new skills such as sharing and taking turns and the activities will provide ways to help them with this.
- Explain that being in this group is a bit different to the rest of school because in here they can choose not to join in the discussions if they do not want to.
- Reflect 'It's really important that you feel happy being in here and sharing your ideas. Some children find this easy, and other children find it difficult and that's because we are all different. It's ok in here if you need help with this and you can just say if you do not want to join in our discussions, but this group is to help make this easier for you to do.'
- If a child is looking round the room then reflect 'I can see you are looking round the room, maybe it feels a bit strange coming in here.'
- Explain that you will see them every week for 6 weeks and if you need to miss a week due to a school trip or you being absent then they will have the session the following week so they will not miss it.
- Tell them you will see them at the same time on the same day each week and show them on the clock the start and end time.
- Give each child a folder and a session chart.
- Encourage them to colour in week one on their chart and say they can choose which colour to use.
- Ask them to put the chart in their folder when they have finished.
- If a child needs help with this reflect 'It can be difficult to do this and I wonder if you would like some help with it?'
- Explain that they can write their name however they want to on their folder as it is theirs and 'you can do it in big or small writing wherever you want to as it's your folder.'
- If a child looks unsure reflect 'It seems like you're not sure where or how to write it, but remember you can choose and there's no right or wrong way.'
- Collect the folders and explain that you will look after then until next week and say 'When you come in next week I will have your folder and colour chart set out waiting for you, just like I did this week.'
- Introduce them to the idea of ground rules for the group and encourage each child to contribute to the group rules if they wish to; allow children to just observe and not contribute if they want to. Reflect 'It can be hard to think of things to say so don't worry if you can't think of a rule today, we will look at this again next week.'
- Write the ground rules for the group on card and display them so all the children can see them easily.
- Explain that the rules will be up each week to help everyone to follow.

Middle (20 minutes)

- Explain that they will be doing an individual poster 'all about me' as they are going to be spending time together over the next six weeks and this can be a way of getting to know more about each other. Reflect 'Sometimes it can be hard to just talk about ourselves and making a poster where we can write or draw things can be an easier way of sharing things about ourselves with each other.'
- Explain that there is no right or wrong way of doing their poster and they may all do it differently as they are all different people.
- Explain that they can write and/or draw and can decide what they would like to put on their poster; e.g. they may want to put things they like and don't like.
- Explain that you would like everyone to share their poster with the group when they have finished and reflect 'This may feel a bit uncomfortable at first as we're just getting to know each other, but I'd like everyone to try and do this.'
- While they are working on their posters ensure you spend equal time acknowledging each child's work.
- Give them a five-minute warning when they will have to finish their posters by, then a one-minute warning, reflecting 'It can be hard to stop when you're working on something, but you need to finish off now.'
- Ask each child to share their poster with the group and encourage them to look at the things that are the same and the things that are different. You can help with this by acknowledging 'Both Paul and Yousef like blue, and everyone seems to dislike Brussels sprouts.'
- Acknowledge that people being different is a positive thing; e.g. 'Imagine if everyone was the same, it would be very boring, it's good that everyone is different and likes different things. Imagine if everyone in the whole school loved football, there would be too many children to play on the team.'
- Introduce the importance of uniqueness by saying 'We are all individuals and that makes us unique, does anyone know what that means?'
- Explain that it means we are all special in our own way and acknowledge 'There is no one else in the world like us and that's what makes us unique.'
- Ask each child to comment on how it felt to share their collage with the group and reflect 'It may be hard to say how we feel sometimes so that's what we're going to practise doing in here.'
- If a child or children doesn't want to share, then reflect 'It seems like it's too hard for you to do this so it's ok not to, you can just listen to the other children say how they feel.'
- Encourage them to put their poster in their folder and remind them that they can take it with them on the last week.
- Reflect 'It can be hard when you've made something and want to take it with you today, but I'm going to keep all your things safe for you in your folder.'

Ending (5 minutes)

- Explain that the session will end in the same way each week by asking them to share something about themselves and this week you will be asking them all to share one thing they like. This is linked to the task they have just done to make it easier for the children to get used to doing this.
- Acknowledge that you have asked them to do lots of sharing about themselves today by reflecting 'I've asked you to share lots of things about yourself today and this may have felt a bit uncomfortable at first, but as we will be doing more of this each week you may get used to it and it may feel more comfortable.'

- Remind them they can choose not to share if they do not want to.
- End the session by saying 'Thank you for sharing about yourselves today, I've enjoyed getting to know you a bit better.'
- Praise them for their hard work in the session and tell them you will see them at the same time and in the same room next week.
- Walk them back to their class.

Overview: week two

Beginning (10 minutes)

- Encourage each child to colour their chart.
- Check whether they remember the ground rules and ask whether they want to add to them.
- Ask them to recall last week's session and what they did.

Middle (25 minutes)

- Explain that this week's activity is about giving compliments and ask if anyone knows what that means and explain or clarify if necessary.
- Set the compliments cards out on the table and read each one out and check they have understood them.
- Give each child a set of compliments and ask them to choose one for each child in the group, complete them and give them to that person.
- Give each child a piece of card and a glue stick to make a poster using the compliments they have received.
- Encourage each child to share what it felt like to give and receive compliments.
- Ask them to think of someone outside the group they can give a compliment to today and encourage them to do this.

Ending (5 minutes)

- Explain that it is the same task as last week, but this week ask each child to say 'I feel'.

Facilitator's guide: week two

Beginning (10 minutes)

- Put each child's folder on the table in the same place as last week and put the ground rules up on the wall.
- Encourage them to find their folder and colour in their session chart.
- Acknowledge that you are pleased to see them all again.
- Encourage them to put their session chart in their folder.
- Show them the start and end time on the clock.
- Ask them whether they can remember the ground rules and show them.
- Ask whether anyone would like to add to the ground rules and remind them it's ok if they don't want to.
- Ask them to recall last week's session and what they did, prompt them if needed and praise them for remembering.

Middle (25 minutes)

- Explain that this week's activity is about giving compliments and ask if anyone knows what the word means; if they look unsure you can acknowledge 'It may be a word that you've heard and are not sure what it means. If I said I like your hair Jessica, then I would be giving Jessica a compliment. A compliment is saying something kind or nice to someone.'
- Explore with them the kind of things you could give people compliments for, e.g. the way someone looks, the kind of person they are, the things they are good at, etc.
- Set the compliments cards (see resources section) out on the table and go through each one ensuring each child understands them.
- If a child looks unsure you can reflect 'I can see you're looking a bit unsure, let me give you an example and that may help you to understand; e.g. I appreciated you staying in at break time to help me tidy the classroom.' Check they have understood.
- Give each child a set of compliments cards and explain they can choose one for each person in the group and complete it; they don't need to use them all.
- Encourage them to come up with their own ideas and remind them you are available for help by acknowledging 'Let me know if you would like some help with spellings as it's not a spelling test in here and it's ok to ask for help if you need it.'
- Encourage each child to give the compliment card to the person it is for.
- Give each child a piece of card and a glue stick to attach the compliments they have received on to the card.
- Encourage the children to share what it felt like to give and receive compliments.
- If a child seems unsure about doing this reflect 'It may have felt uncomfortable when you looked at your compliments and it may be hard to say how that felt, but I'm wondering whether it felt nice or strange or any other word when you looked at the compliments you'd been given.'
- When they have all shared how it felt, acknowledge some of the words they used by saying 'So giving people compliments can make them feel good, happy, special, etc. I would like you to think about someone outside the group, it can be anyone you choose and give them a compliment today. Now we all know how good it feels to give and to get compliments, it would be nice for us to try and do it more.'
- Encourage them to put their compliments sheet in their folder and remind them they can take it with them on the last week.
- Reflect 'It can be hard when you've made something and want to take it with you today, but I'm going to keep all your things safe for you in your folder.'

Ending (5 minutes)

- Explain that the ending for this week will involve them sharing something about themselves and this week you will be asking them all to share how they feel.
- Remind them they can choose not to share if they do not want to.
- Start with a different child to last week and praise each child individually for sharing how they feel with the group.
- Praise them for their hard work in the session and tell them you will see them at the same time and in the same room next week.
- Walk them back to their class.

Overview: week three

Beginning (10 minutes)

- Encourage each child to colour their chart.
- Check whether they remember the ground rules and ask whether they want to add to them.
- Ask them to recall last week's session and what they did.

Middle (25 minutes)

- Explain that each child will be making a poem using the letters of their name.
- Give each child a piece of card and ask them to write their name on it with space underneath to write a word vertically.
- Encourage each child to think of a word to describe themselves for each letter of their name, e.g. C for caring, and write this under the relevant letter of their name.
- Encourage them to help each other think of words if they need help.
- Ask them to decorate them if they want to.
- Encourage them to hold up their poems and share them with the group.
- Encourage each child to give the child a compliment about their poem when they are holding it up.
- Encourage each child to say how it feels to share their poem with the group.

Ending (5 minutes)

Explain that it is the same task as last week, but this week it is 'I enjoy'.

Facilitator's guide: week three

Beginning (10 minutes)

- Put each child's folder on the table in the same place as last week and put the ground rules up on the wall.
- Encourage them to find their folder and colour in their session chart.
- Acknowledge that you are pleased to see them all again.
- Encourage them to put their session chart in their folder.
- Show them the start and end time on the clock.
- Ask them whether they can remember the ground rules and show them.
- Ask whether anyone would like to add to the ground rules and remind them it's ok if they don't want to.
- Ask them to recall last week's session and what they did, prompt them if needed and praise them for remembering.
- Ask them if they remembered to give a compliment to someone and if they did would anyone like to share what they did.
- If a child didn't remember to do this reflect 'It can be difficult to remember things outside the group as school can be so busy, but maybe you can try again this week if you would like to.

Middle (25 minutes)

- Explain that each child will be doing a poem using the letters of their name. It is useful for you to spend some time before the group to ensure you can think of a word for each letter of the child's name; e.g. Zuleika or Queenie may be more difficult for you to do on the spot.
- Give each child some card and explain they will be thinking of a word to describe themselves for each letter of their name.
- Acknowledge 'There is no right or wrong way of doing this, it's your poem and you can do it however you want to.'
- If a child looks anxious reflect 'This may seem like it's a difficult thing to do but we can all help each other to think of words if we get stuck.'
- Acknowledge 'You may need some help from an adult with this, and I can help if you would like me to.'
- Tell them when they have five minutes and then one minute left so they are able to manage the time.
- If a child finishes before the others they can decorate the poem if they wish to.
- Encourage each child to hold them up for the rest of the group to look at and ask each child to think of a compliment they could give to the others when they do this. Reflect 'I know it can sometimes be hard to think of compliments to give, but remember when we talked about this last week and let's see if we're able to do this.'
- If a child doesn't want to hold their poem up you can reflect 'Maybe it feels too difficult to do that; I wonder how it would feel if I held it up for you?'
- If the child still looks uncomfortable then reflect 'Maybe that would still feel too difficult and that's ok, you can pass on this if you want to.'
- Encourage each child to say how it felt to share their poem with the group.
- Encourage them to put their poem in their folder and remind them that they can take it with them on the last week.
- Reflect 'It can be hard when you've made something and want to take it with you today, but I'm going to keep all your things safe for you in your folder.'

Ending (5 minutes)

- Explain that this week you will end the session by sharing something about you that you enjoy.
- Remind them they can choose not to share if they do not want to.
- Start with a different child so they all have a turn to go first.
- Praise them for their hard work in the session and tell them you will see them at the same time and in the same room next week.
- Walk them back to their class.

Overview: week four

Beginning (10 minutes)

- Encourage each child to colour their chart.
- Check whether they remember the ground rules and ask whether they want to add to them.
- Ask them to recall last week's session and what they did.

Middle (25 minutes)

- Introduce the concept of praise by asking the group what it means and give examples to clarify if necessary.
- Encourage them to share examples of when they have been praised and discuss how it feels.
- Explain that they will be making their own praise booklet and give them out.
- Encourage them to complete them and share one example from their book with the group.
- Encourage each child to say how it feels to do this.

Ending (5 minutes)

- Explain that it is the same task as last week, but this week it is 'I am'.

Facilitator's guide: week four

Beginning (10 minutes)

- Put each child's folder on the table in the same place as last week and put the ground rules up on the wall.
- Encourage them to find their folder and colour in their session chart.
- Acknowledge that you are pleased to see them all again.
- Encourage them to put their session chart in their folder.
- Show them the start and end time on the clock.
- Ask them whether they can remember the ground rules and show them.
- Ask whether anyone would like to add to the ground rules and remind them it's ok if they don't want to.
- Ask them to recall last week's session and what they did, prompt them if needed and praise them for remembering.

Middle (25 minutes)

- Introduce the concept of praise by asking the group what it means.
- If they are unsure you can give examples such as 'If I say well done for working hard on your picture, I wonder if that would be praise?'
- Encourage them to share examples of when they have been praised by saying 'I wonder if we can think of things that we have been praised for?'
- Encourage each child to share an example with the group if they feel comfortable doing this.

- Encourage them to share how it feels to be praised by asking 'I wonder how it feels when people say kind things to us?'
- Explain that they will be making their own praise book (see resources section) and give them out to each child.
- Remind them that you are there to help them if they need it by acknowledging 'Remember I am here to help you and it is not a spelling test so I can help you to spell any words you may need help with.'
- Ask them to write their name on the front cover and complete the first page 'To praise someone means' in their own words.
- If a child appears to be finding this difficult, encourage them by saying 'I wonder if you can remember what we said it means to praise someone?
- If they are still finding this difficult then tell them.
- Ask them to turn to the next page 'I have been praised for' and ask them to complete this; explain that they can use the example they shared with the group before or think of another one.
- The children may be working at different speeds so give permission for the children who are working faster to continue working through the book at their own pace if they would like to.
- Remind them you are there to help them and that it would also be kind if they could help each other if they are able to.
- Ensure you monitor each child in the group as they may need help with some of the pages.
- Reflect 'It may feel uncomfortable to think about something you would like to be praised for, but this can be anything at all; it's your praise book and you can choose what you would like to put in it.'
- When they get to the last page 'I have praised someone for', explain that they can use an example of when they have done this or they could think of something they would like to praise someone for.
- If a child appears to need help with this you can reflect 'It may be difficult to think of an example for this one; I wonder whether you can think of how you could praise someone in this group?'
- If some children finish the book before the others they can decorate the front cover if they would like to.
- When they have all finished the books encourage each child to choose one page they would be happy to share with the rest of the group and read them out.
- If a child appears reluctant to do this then reflect 'Maybe it feels uncomfortable sharing your examples; I wonder if I could help you with this? How would you feel about me reading it out to the group?'
- If the child is still unsure then give them permission to pass by acknowledging 'Sometimes it can feel too difficult to share things about ourselves, and that's ok; in here we don't have to read things out or share our thoughts if we don't want to.'
- Ask the group how they felt about sharing their ideas with the group and praise them for doing this.
- Encourage them all to try and praise other people during the week and see how it feels for them to do this.
- Encourage them to put their praise book in their folder and remind them that they can take it with them on the last week.
- Reflect 'It can be hard when you've made something and want to take it with you today, but I'm going to keep all your things safe for you in your folder.'

Ending (5 minutes)

- Explain that the ending for this week will involve them sharing something about themselves and this week you will be asking them all to say a sentence starting with 'I am'.
- Remind them they can choose not to share if they do not want to.
- Encourage them to help each other to remember to praise someone and say that you will remind them if you see them.
- Praise them for their hard work in the session and tell them you will see them at the same time and in the same room next week.
- Walk them back to their class.

Overview: week five

Beginning (10 minutes)

- Encourage each child to colour their chart.
- Check whether they remember the ground rules and ask whether they want to add to them.
- Ask them to recall last week's session and what they did.

Middle (25 minutes)

- Explain that this week they will be looking at different situations that may happen and work in pairs to decide what they would do in each situation.
- Give each pair two different scenarios and encourage them to work together on how they would feel and how they would respond.
- Encourage the whole group to discuss all the scenarios and how they felt about each situation.

Ending (5 minutes)

- Explain that it is the same task as last week, but this week it is 'I think'.

Facilitator's guide: week five

Beginning (10 minutes)

- Put each child's folder on the table in the same place as last week and put the ground rules up on the wall.
- Encourage them to find their folder and colour in their session chart.
- Acknowledge that you are pleased to see them all again.
- Encourage them to put their session chart in their folder.
- Show them the start and end time on the clock.
- Ask them whether they can remember the ground rules and show them.
- Ask whether anyone would like to add to the ground rules and remind them it's ok if they don't want to.
- Ask them to recall last week's session and what they did, prompt them if needed and praise them for remembering; ask them whether they remembered to praise people and how this felt if they did this.

● Acknowledge the children who did this and reflect to the children who didn't by saying 'It can be difficult to remember to do things outside the group and it's ok if you didn't remember to do it, but maybe you could try and do it this week if you would like to.'

Middle (25 minutes)

● Explain that this week they will be looking at different situations that may happen and working in pairs to decide how they would feel and what they may do in each situation, and then you will discuss each one with the whole group.

● Put them in pairs with a child they haven't worked with before, ensuring there is a balance of a confident with a less confident child if possible.

● Explain they have five minutes to discuss each scenario and that you will tell them when to move on to the second one.

● Acknowledge that this is a different task to the other tasks they have done so far in the group and reflect 'It may be that you need some help from an adult with this task and I can help you if you need it. Remember there are no right or wrong answers to this task.'

● Give each pair two different scenarios (see resources section) and read through them with each pair away from the other pair if possible so they will not be disturbed.

● Spend time with each pair equally and encourage them to discuss each one and think about how they may feel by reflecting 'I'm wondering how that would feel for that person; I wonder how it would feel to see that happening to someone.'

● Acknowledge that each person in the pair may feel differently and want to respond differently and that's ok, they can share what they both think. Reflect 'You may not both think or feel the same and that's ok as you're different people; you can share what you both think with the group.'

● Ensure you manage the time for them by encouraging them to move on to the second scenario after half the time has gone; e.g. 'Just a couple more minutes on this one and then you need to move on to the next scenario.'

● Encourage each pair to take it in turns to share a scenario with you reading it out to the group and each pair sharing how they felt, what they would do and why.

● Encourage the pair who didn't work on the scenario to comment if they wish to.

● Validate their responses to each situation by acknowledging their feelings; e.g. 'I can see that it would make you feel angry if someone was being made fun of (scenario 1). I can see that it would make you feel jealous if someone got something you wanted (scenario 4).

● Praise the group for their thoughtful responses at the end of the discussion by acknowledging 'You all worked very hard thinking about how you felt and what you would do in each of those situations, well done.'

Ending (5 minutes)

● Acknowledge that next week will be the last week and reflect 'It may feel a bit sad as we've worked together for a while and I've enjoyed getting to know you all a bit more than I did before we had our group.'

● Explain that the ending for this week will involve them sharing something about themselves and this week you will be asking them all to say a sentence starting with 'I think'.

● Remind them they can choose not to share if they do not want to.

● Start with a different child so they all have a turn to go first.

● Praise them for their hard work in the session and tell them you will see them at the same time and in the same room next week.

● Walk them back to their class.

Overview: week six

Beginning (10 minutes)

- Encourage each child to colour their chart.
- Check whether they remember the ground rules and ask whether they want to add to them.
- Recap each week and encourage them to remember the activities and tasks they have carried out.

Middle (25 minutes)

- Explain that they have each won an award and encourage them to identify what they won the award for.
- Ask each child to complete their own award certificate and pass it to the person next to them to complete the second section of an award for their contribution to the group, e.g. sharing, being kind, etc.
- Ask each child to share their award certificate with the group and encourage them to listen and clap and cheer when they have finished.

Ending (5 minutes)

- Explain that this week you will end the session by sharing something you have liked about being in the group.
- Give each child their folder and explain that they can take it with them if they would like to.
- Acknowledge how hard they have all worked and how much you have enjoyed spending time with them.

Facilitator's guide: week six

Beginning (10 minutes)

- Put each child's folder on the table in the same place as last week and put the ground rules up on the wall.
- Encourage them to find their folder and colour in their session chart.
- Acknowledge that you are pleased to see them all again.
- Encourage them to put their session chart in their folder.
- Show them the start and end time on the clock.
- Ask them whether they can remember the ground rules and show them.
- Ask whether anyone would like to add to the ground rules and remind them it's ok if they don't want to.
- Remind them that this is their last week and respond appropriately to any comments they make; e.g. 'I know it may feel sad as we've worked together for six weeks.'
- Recap each week and encourage them to remember the activities. You may want to have a list with you to help you to remember.
- While they are doing this you can acknowledge any memorable moments for you; e.g. 'I remember when you did the compliments activity and you were all really good at thinking of kind things to say to each other.'
- Respond appropriately to any comments the children make about any memories they have by reflecting 'I hear you've got some good memories of our time together in the group too.'

Middle (25 minutes)

- Explain that they have each won an award and encourage them to think about what they've won it for. Acknowledge 'It can be anything you choose, it may be something you did in this group or around school or for another person, it can be anything.'
- Give each child an award certificate and encourage them to think of what they want to put and explain that the second section will be completed by the person who is sitting next to them.
- If a child appears unsure or anxious reflect 'It can be hard to think about something we've done well but remember it can be anything at all.'
- Explain the second section is for them to think about what that person did in the group that was helpful, kind, thoughtful, etc.
- Ask them to pass it on to the person sitting next to them to complete the second section of the award certificate for their contribution to the group.
- If a child appears unsure about this you can encourage them by reflecting 'I can see you're not sure what to put; would it help to think about all the activities we did again as that may help you to think of something.'
- Ask each child to share their award certificate with the group and encourage the other children to clap and cheer when they have finished.

Ending (5 minutes)

- Explain that this week you will end the session by sharing something you have liked about being in the group.
- Remind them they can choose not to share if they do not want to.
- Give each child their folder and explain that they can take it with them if they would like to.
- If a child doesn't want to take their folder reflect 'Maybe you're unsure about taking it back to class with you; you can collect it from the reception at home time if you would prefer to.'
- Acknowledge that 'Sometimes endings can feel sad and I have really enjoyed spending time with you all and you've all worked very hard in here. Although we won't have our group anymore we will still see each other around school, which I know won't be the same, but you can always come and talk to me if you want to.'

Conclusion

The impact that good educational practice can have on children and families is invaluable. I hope I have demonstrated that schools have a crucial role to play in developing positive mental health and well-being in children, and the prevention of further difficulties in adult life and problems for society as a whole. Our prisons and mental health systems have a large percentage of adults who had difficult early experiences as children, which they have carried into their adult lives. We have a responsibility as a society to break the perpetuation of that cycle by providing opportunities for the next generation of young people to have experiences that promote positive mental health and well-being. There are endless possibilities throughout the school day to introduce emotional vocabulary, provide children with skills and opportunities to express their feelings and produce experiences that enable them to learn about their emotional health and well-being. When we meet children's emotional and social needs we remove the barriers that create blockages and enable them to learn.

The group work programme is an ideal opportunity to do this in a way that can be easily integrated into the school day with minimal disruption and maximum success. It enables schools to do things differently and provide children with opportunities to experience new ways of understanding and managing their feelings. As adults we may try to protect children from experiencing sadness, hurt and upset, but these are part of life along with happiness, joy and excitement. Our task as practitioners is to support children with experiencing all feelings, not just some feelings.

Every child deserves to be happy, safe and settled in school and have the skills to build friendships, the confidence to do well and the opportunity to reach their full potential. Children need the opportunity to feel they belong, are worthwhile, have something to offer and can make a contribution to the world. Children need to feel they have a purpose in the same way as adults do.

We've got to get it right for children from now. There are generations of children who have had negative experiences of school, resulting in negative views of themselves and taking those experiences into adulthood, therefore increasing the likelihood of ending up in our prisons or mental health systems, having children of their own and repeating the cycle. The long-term consequences for individuals, families and society as a whole of children being emotionally unhealthy and having poor relational skills are enormous. We need to take children's mental health seriously. If we invest in children's emotional health and well-being we provide them with potential skills for life; if we don't we provide them with potential problems for life.

Resources

This section contains all the resources needed to prepare, plan and evaluate the group work programmes. These can be photocopied and prepared in advance of the programme. The resources include:

- guidelines for completing intervention questionnaires
- start and end of intervention questionnaires
- a completed example of a group work report
- a blank format of a group work report
- a register
- session notes to be completed at the end of each session
- a door sign

Resources for delivering friendship group:

- overall resources list
- child session chart to be completed each week
- understanding differences questionnaire
- jealousy story and accompanying questions
- 'I have enjoyed' slips
- box template

Resources for delivering self-esteem:

- overall resources list
- child session chart to be completed each week
- compliments slips
- praise book
- scenarios
- award certificate

Group work questionnaires guidelines for group facilitators

- Ask the child's class teacher or teaching assistant to complete the start questionnaires for each child that will be in the group with you.
- Ensure they complete each question and include additional comments about the child and how they are generally in class, at break times and around school. For example, Kevin can be quiet and withdrawn at times or Mia finds it hard to wait her turn and is frequently fighting with other children at lunchtime.
- Ask the same person to complete the end questionnaire for each child, ensuring they complete the section about any other changes that have occurred. For example, Kevin is more confident and is sharing his ideas more in class or Mia is being more patient and is gradually developing more friendships with the other children in the class.
- Compare each question using the start and end questionnaire for each child.
- Identify any positive changes that have occurred in the scoring; for example, a child who could take turns only sometimes but is now able to frequently, along with any comments from the person who completed the end questionnaire.
- List the positive changes and write a paragraph describing how you experienced the child in the group sessions; for example, at first Jamie found it difficult to follow the group rules and kept interrupting while the other children were talking. However, after several gentle reminders and support from the group he was able to do this more easily. He became more confident at sharing his feelings and was able to acknowledge that he felt sad that the group was finishing.

Group work start of intervention questionnaire

Child's name:
Date of birth:

Please complete the following questions based on your knowledge of the child during the last month:

	Yes	No	Sometimes
Is this child able to share?			
Is this child able to make friends easily?			
Is this child kind to other children?			
Is this child able to take turns?			
Does this child have friends?			
Is this child popular?			
Does this child have conflicts with other children?			
Does this child bully other children?			
Does this child do what adults ask?			
Does this child offer to help?			
Does this child tell lies?			
Does this child find it difficult to concentrate?			
Does this child focus and engage with their learning?			
Does this child fidget and appear restless?			
Does this child appear to be anxious, worried or scared?			
Does this child have angry outbursts or tantrums?			
Is this child able to express their feelings easily?			
Does this child appear to be confident?			
Does this child say they feel unwell?			
Does this child appear to be happy?			

Any other comments:

Signed:
Date:

Group work end of intervention questionnaire

Child's name:

Date of birth:

Please complete the following questions based on your knowledge of the child during the last two weeks:

	Yes	No	Sometimes
Is this child able to share?			
Is this child able to make friends easily?			
Is this child kind to other children?			
Is this child able to take turns?			
Does this child have friends?			
Is this child popular?			
Does this child have conflicts with other children?			
Does this child bully other children?			
Does this child do what adults ask?			
Does this child offer to help?			
Does this child tell lies?			
Does this child find it difficult to concentrate?			
Does this child focus and engage with their learning?			
Does this child fidget and appear restless?			
Does this child appear to be anxious, worried or scared?			
Does this child have angry outbursts or tantrums?			
Is this child able to express their feelings easily?			
Does this child appear to be confident?			
Does this child say they feel unwell?			
Does this child appear to be happy?			

Any other changes that have occurred:

Signed:

Date:

Group work report

Child's name:	Jodie Bracken
Date of birth:	25. 6. 03
Type of group:	Friendship
Group facilitator:	Nathan Crompton
Group dates:	January–February 2012

Questionnaire evaluation:

The questionnaires show that Jodie has made several positive changes since being in the group. She is able to share more easily and is being kinder to other children. Her friendships have improved and she is now more popular. She is no longer telling lies which she was sometimes doing before the group sessions. Her concentration has improved and she is less restless.

Staff comments:

Her class teacher is very pleased with the progress Jodie has made and has noticed that her friendships have improved. She feels she is more confident now and seems to be happier in herself.

Facilitator's comments:

Jodie was a bit quiet and anxious at the start of the group work sessions. She appeared to be worried about making mistakes and would wait for the other children to start before beginning the activity. However, with lots of reassurance she gradually became more confident and started sharing her thoughts and ideas. Her friendships with the other children in the group developed as the sessions progressed.

Recommendations:

Jodie may still need support to help her manage her anxiety about getting things wrong from her class teacher and other adults in school.

Signed:

Date:

© Cath Hunter, *Understanding and Managing Children's Behaviour through Group Work Ages 7–11*, Routledge, 2013

Group work report

Child's name:	
Date of birth:	
Type of group:	
Group facilitator:	
Group dates:	
Questionnaire evaluation:	
Staff comments:	
Facilitator's comments:	
Recommendations:	
Signed:	
Date:	

Group work register

Please record the date that each group work session takes place and tick whether or not the child attended.

Name of child	Date	Date	Date	Date	Date	Date

Signed ....

Print name ....

Date ....

Group work session notes

Group work facilitator ....

Type of group ....

Date	Session number	Session detail and comments (it is useful to make notes on individual children and group dynamics)

Door sign

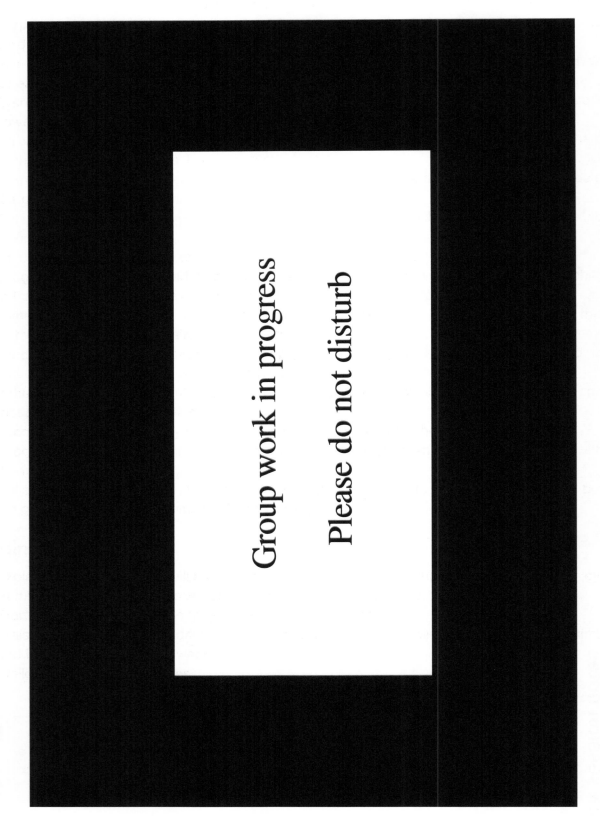

Group work in progress

Please do not disturb

Friendship resources

Resources for friendship group

- Clock
- Register and session record (to be completed each week)
- Stickers for children's names if needed (week one)
- Folders for each child (all the same colour)
- Weekly chart for each child
- Felt pens
- Graphite and coloured pencils
- Scissors for each child (week four)
- Glue sticks for each child (week four)
- Large card for ground rules
- A4 white card (week three)
- Blu tack for ground rules
- A3 white paper (week one)
- A3 card (week four)
- Collage materials (week four)
- Four envelopes and paper (week five)
- Boxes (see week six template)
- A4 white paper (week six)
- Understanding differences questionnaire (week two)
- Jealousy story and question (week five)
- 'I have enjoyed working with you' worksheet (week six)

Session chart

Understanding differences interview

Ask your friend the following questions:

- What is your name?

- How old are you?

- What is your favourite colour?

- What is your favourite thing to do?

- What is your favourite food?

- What makes you happy?

- What makes you sad?

- One thing we both like doing is …

- One thing my new friend could teach me …

Emily feels jealous

It was the day of the class assembly and Emily was excited to see who had been chosen to read their poem out to the rest of the school. She felt sure it would be her and was imagining standing at the front while everyone clapped and cheered her. She was woken suddenly from her daydream by her baby sister crying in her cot. Emily loved Sophie but wished she wouldn't cry so much or take up so much attention. Since Sophie had been born it felt like everyone had forgotten about Emily, apart from when they were telling her to be a 'good girl and fetch a nappy' or 'not to make a fuss'. Sometimes Emily wished Sophie could go and live somewhere else so it could just be her, mum and dad again, just like the old days.

Emily got dressed and tried to ignore Sophie's crying until her mum called to her, 'I won't be a minute, just talk to her till I come in.' Emily didn't want to talk to her, what was the point, she couldn't talk back, she'd just make gurgling noises that her mum and dad thought were amazing, but Emily thought were boring and stupid. If only she could have an older sister like her friend Marie. Marie's older sister Clare was great fun and took Marie shopping and to the cinema. 'It's not fair,' thought Emily, 'I wish I had an older sister instead of a boring baby one.'

Just then mum came into the room; she looked really tired as she had done all the time since Sophie had been born. By this time Sophie was standing up in her cot and screaming, her face looked like a raspberry that was about to explode thought Emily and started smiling to herself. 'I don't know what you're smiling about,' said mum, 'it's not funny, now go and get her bottle from downstairs while I change her.'

As Emily ran through the school gates she was delighted to see Marie waiting for her. 'I can't wait till assembly,' she said, 'I think Mrs O'Neill will chose my poem to read out' as she linked Marie's arm and walked to class with her. The poem had been set for homework last week and Emily was really pleased with hers. While Mrs O'Neill took the register Emily could hardly sit still; she had butterflies in her stomach and couldn't stop smiling. Jonathan Grainger, who was always picking his nose, noticed and smiled back and even this didn't stop her smiling.

'The winner of the poem competition is …' announced Mrs O'Neill, '… Marie James.' The whole class started clapping and Emily could feel her bottom lip wobbling. How could it not be hers, she'd worked so hard on it and Marie had just rushed hers as she was going out for pizza with her sister Clare that night. Emily found it difficult to clap and tried hard to smile across at Marie who was beaming. 'Marie will read her poem to the whole school in assembly this afternoon,' said Mrs O'Neill.

By lunchtime Emily was feeling angry, very angry; why should Marie's poem win the competition – Marie had everything. As they walked back to class all the other children were chatting excitedly to Marie, 'She doesn't even need me as a friend anymore,' thought Emily. She walked into the class and realised she was the first one to arrive; she ran over to Marie's drawer, took her poem out and shoved it underneath a pile of papers in Jonathan's drawer. That'll show her, she thought. She just had time to close the drawer as the other children arrived.

It was time for assembly and Marie started rummaging in her drawer. 'Where's my poem? I can't find it, it's not here,' shouted Marie looking close to tears.

Questions for discussion

1 Why did Emily want to have an older sister?

2 Who was Emily jealous of?

3 Why was Emily jealous?

4 What do you think will happen next?

5 What could Emily have done to stop feeling like this?

6 Have you ever felt jealous or left out?

7 What could you do next time you feel like this?

I have enjoyed working with you in this group because

I have enjoyed working with you in this group because

I have enjoyed working with you in this group because

I have enjoyed working with you in this group because

I have enjoyed working with you in this group because

I have enjoyed working with you in this group because

I have enjoyed working with you in this group because

Box template

Self-esteem resources

Resources for self-esteem group

- Clock
- Register and session record (to be completed each week)
- Stickers for children's names if needed (week one)
- Folders for each child (all the same colour)
- Weekly chart for each child
- Felt pens
- Lead and coloured pencils
- Glue sticks for each child (week two)
- Large card for ground rules
- Blu tack for ground rules
- Coloured card (week two, week three)
- A4 white paper (week one)
- Compliments worksheet (week two)
- Praise booklet (week four)
- Scenarios (week five)
- Award certificate (week six)

Session chart

I really like you because

I like your

I like it when you

I appreciated when you

You are great at

You are special because

Congratulations for

I like the way you

My Praise Book

Name ....

To praise someone means

I have been praised for

When I get praised I feel

Something I would like to be praised for is

I have praised someone for

Scenarios

1 All your friends are laughing at and making fun of someone's new shoes.

   ● How do you feel?
   ● What would you do and why?

2 Your class teacher is absent and you have a supply teacher for the day. Some of the class are misbehaving, being rude and pretending they sit in different seats to their own.

   ● How do you feel?
   ● What would you do and why?

3 All your friends are changing to packed lunches and will be moving to a different table in the dinner hall, but you really enjoy having school dinners.

   ● How do you feel?
   ● What would you do and why?

4 Your brother or sister gets something for Christmas that you have really wanted for a long time.

   ● How do you feel?
   ● What would you do and why?

AWARD CERTIFICATE

This award is presented to

For being

And for contributing to the group by

Index

Page numbers in **bold** indicate tables and in *italics* indicate figures.